James Martineau

Home Prayers

With two services for public worship

James Martineau

Home Prayers
With two services for public worship

ISBN/EAN: 9783337034450

Printed in Europe, USA, Canada, Australia, Japan

Cover: Foto ©Lupo / pixelio.de

More available books at **www.hansebooks.com**

HOME PRAYERS,

WITH

TWO SERVICES

FOR

PUBLIC WORSHIP.

BY

JAMES MARTINEAU.

Second Edition.

When ye pray, say, Our Father.—LUKE xi. 2.

LONDON:
LONGMANS, GREEN AND CO.
AND NEW YORK: 15, EAST 16TH STREET
1892.

LONDON:
PRINTED BY WOODFALL AND KINDER,
70 TO 76, LONG ACRE, W.C.

PREFACE.

As this small volume is the last which I shall offer to my contemporaries, so is it the first of which I cannot render any distinct account. In all previous cases I have had something to say which it seemed needful to throw into the courses of current thought; and I could indicate the place into which it might naturally flow. For the following pages I can offer no such plea. They add nothing to the common stock of human experience. They pour forth only the story of every inward life, and breathe the old familiar tones of wonder, sorrow and aspiration. They do but utter some little part of what every one may lay bare for himself before Him that seeth in secret. What excuse then can there be for any attempt, on another's part, to say it for him? So deeply have I always felt the force of this question, as hitherto to shrink from sending 'Prayers to the press;—both as a vicarious intermeddling with the free devotion of souls unknown, and as a gratuitous exposure of a sacred confidence between the personal conscience and the Searcher of hearts. Thus regarded, *published* Prayers seemed at variance with the injunction,—" Thou, when thou prayest, enter into thine inner chamber, and *having shut the door*, pray to thy Father who is in secret."

I own, however, to some gradual softening of this scruple. Perhaps it may be the declining strength of life which induces a natural sympathy with the varieties of mental dependence that cannot even confess their helplessness without interpreter;—the child's scanty conscience and unready mood;—the wandering thoughts of the untrained mind;—the slow compunctions of the self-satisfied;—the dry affections of the too prosperous. At all events I am more aware than I was of the need of *fellowship* in the spiritual life, and less disposed to trust to its pure spontaneity; and therefore deem it no longer a breach of true reserve, but rather a requital for many a blessed incentive from souls and books that have uplifted me, if, standing on the last verge of this scene of things, I treat it as my Confessional, and bear witness to others, ere I go, how its vicissitudes and possibilities have looked to me and have borrowed their true significance from the eternal light of God beyond the veil. If even a few persons who fancy themselves alone shall find here an echo of their heart-tones or genuine words for what falters upon their lips, their scattered feeling after the true notes may swell into a chorus, and out of faint beginnings rise into a glow of faith. So easily lost are the tender voices of the spirit, that we need to overhear each other.

The 'Home Prayers' which form the chief part of this volume are thrown into the shape suitable for a plurality of persons assembled to use them. But, with slight exception, they are equally available for individual devotion, by the simplest modification of grammatical form. So far as it is possible for one person to speak for many, the needs of each are the needs of all: so that there is no ground for any substantive difference between the manuals of personal and those of collective devotion. The specialties of individual trial and temptation, despondency and joy, are of infinite variety, and can only be met by the spontaneous piety stirred in each by the discipline of life. The pathetic cries which are thus wrung from the heart of almost every lot supplement and intensify in meaning the universal language of self-surrender, and quicken it with penetrating power.

The two 'Public Services' which close the volume are reproduced, with some slight modification, from the "Common Prayer for Christian Worship," published in 1862. It was suggested to me that they would be acceptable in Country Houses so placed as to be beyond reach of congenial Church

Worship; and might, in such cases, facilitate the gathering together of neighbours ready for religious sympathy as well as social kindliness. If in ever so few instances they should thus check the growing neglect of Public Worship or the dissentient attendance upon it, I shall be grateful to the friends who have asked for this Appendix to my volume.

I have, in conclusion, to tender my thanks to my friends the Rev. Russell Lant Carpenter, B.A., for permission to use the Prayer on p. 86, which had been contributed to his sister Mary's "Morning and Evening Meditations," 4th Edition, 1857; and Miss Frances Power Cobbe, for similar permission in regard to the Prayer on p. 89, which had its first place in her "Alone to the Alone," 1871.

LONDON, *November* 13, 1891.

CONTENTS.

HOME PRAYERS.

	PAGE
MORNING	1
EVENING	32
———— PENITENTIAL PRAYER	42
MORNING OR EVENING	45
———————————— PENITENTIAL	92
FIRST ASSEMBLING AFTER DEATH OF A HEAD OF THE FAMILY	95

PUBLIC WORSHIP.

PRAYER ON THE OPENING OF A NEW PLACE OF WORSHIP	98
FIRST COMPLETE SERVICE	103
SECOND	121
COLLECTS FOR MORNING AND EVENING	138

MORNING.

SOURCE of all good! Day by day are thy blessings renewed to us: and how should our thanksgivings cease? Our fathers rejoiced to sing thy praise; and from their children's offering thou wilt not turn away. The rest of night, the light of day we gratefully receive as thy gifts, and would dedicate to the service of thy will. O that we too could be re-born like the morning, and our love rise as fresh as the dawn, and our obedience be as sure as the path of the sun! For, as we commune with thee, many shadows from the past dim the joy of thy presence. When we remember our thoughtless lives, our impatient tempers, our selfish aims, we know that thou hast left us without excuse. Thou hast neither made us blind, like the creatures that have no sin; nor left us without holy guidance;

thy still small voice speaking in our inmost conscience; and thine open word having dwelt among us, full of grace and truth, appealing to us to choose the better part. We are not our own, and are ashamed to have lived unto ourselves. Thou hast formed us for thy service; and we must hide our face, that we have shrunk from the glorious hardness of our task. Our daily work has not been wrought as in thy sight. The trials of our patience we have received as earthly pains of nature, not as the heavenly discipline of faith; and the fulness of thy bounties has come to us as dead comfort, not as the living touch of thy love. O true and only God! we have lived in a bondage to the world which bringeth no content; and the passions we serve are as strange idols that cannot deliver. Awake, O Arm of the Lord! and burst our bonds asunder: and take us to serve thee in newness of spirit. May we dread above all the poisoned sweetness of sin, and choose rather the bitterest draughts of healthful duty.

The cup which our Father hath given us, shall we not drink it?

O Thou discerner of thoughts! May we not fall into the snares of a self-deceiving mind. When our holy resolves spring up, may they not wither away because there is no deepness of earth: but, O Thou Lord of the harvest, enrich the furrows of our nature, and hide thy good seed from the cares of this world, and nourish it with the dews of thy pure grace. Humbled by our past infirmities, may we lean no more on our own strength, unsanctified by the memory of thee. May a constant sense of thy presence give us a composed and reverent soul, open our lips with thoughtful and quiet words, fill us with great and gentle thoughts, and sweep away with a holy breath every dust of care, every trace of fear, and every taint of an uncharitable mind.

O God of future years! our age is nothing unto thee. We are here this morning: ere eventide, we may be gone and sunk into the shadows. Our life is as a dream, when one awaketh. May we be as those that lie in wait for the dawning: and when we awake, may we still be with thee. For time and for eternity we commit ourselves to thee, O Lord. Amen.

MORNING.

O GOD of Infinite Holiness, whose we are, and whose perfect will we desire to serve! Be with us now, not with thine outward presence only, but with thy searching and cleansing Spirit, while we dedicate ourselves anew to the work which thou layest on our conscience and our heart. What are we, O Lord, that thou shouldst call us to be witnesses of thy righteousness, and open to us a place in the train of the faithful and saintly who labour and live for thee in every age? Unless thou keep watch over us, and cast us down with thy rebuke, and lift us by thy purifying grace, we can think nothing, love nothing, know nothing, as we ought; and thy Divine light will but be quenched as it passes through our souls. Scatter, O God, the darkness of sense and self within us. Ever looking unto thee, may we more and more gain the single eye, the trusting mind, the fervent spirit, and the heart of willing sacrifice.

Eternal Father, the stay of all our generations, in whose hands our times are! We bless thee for the many sweet and solemn memories that surround us in our time and place, and win us to love the simplicity of wisdom and the beauty of holiness. Awaken us to feel how great a thing it is to live at the end of so many ages, heirs to the thoughts of the wise, the labours of the good, the prayers of the devout. Gather and kindle their power in our hearts; and as we muse upon them, may their fire burn and consume whatever is mean and low within us. Make us one with those who have been touched with pity for the sins and sorrows of the world, and willing, by the free offering of ourselves, to fill up the measure of the sufferings of Christ.

And now, Lord, what wait we for? Only for thy blessing to attend our common life of duty here. Make it all an earnest search for a nearer walk with thee. We know not what a day may bring forth: fill us with steadfast diligence to turn each moment to account; with vigilance against every temptation to indolent, careless, or disordered ways; with unswerving love of whatever things are pure and true: and then may we be without care, as those whose refuge is in thee. Thus make us true followers of him whose meat it was to do thy will and finish thy work. Amen.

MORNING.

O GOD, Allseeing but Unseen! Thou only source of peace and holiness! into thy secret place take us for a moment, and fill us with thy pure and solemn light. We would not go without thy blessing on our way, or mingle with the haste of life without thy clear directing Spirit in our hearts. We are weak, O Lord, and renounce the vain trust in ourselves alone: we are blind, and know not what the hours may bring. But we rest in thee, who never leavest or forsakest us: and whatever we are called to do or suffer, we would put our hand in thine, and freely go where thou mayst lead.

O Searcher of hearts! Thou knowest us better than we know ourselves, and seest the sins which our sinfulness hides from us. Yet even our own conscience beareth witness against us, that we often slumber on our appointed watch; that we are drawn aside by sense and self from the straight and narrow way; that we walk not always lovingly with each other and humbly with thee; that we fear what is not terrible and wish what is not holy in thy sight; and withhold that entire sacrifice of ourselves to thy perfect will, without which we are not crucified with Christ or sharers in his redemption. O look upon our contrition and lift up our weakness, Father of exhaustless mercies! and let the day-spring yet arise within our hearts and bring us healing, strength and joy.

Lord of our life and Disposer of our lot! Thou hast set us in a world glorious with blessed hopes, but sad with many sins and sorrows. O touch us with thine own compassion, and render us organs of thy saving power, to make it ready for thy kingdom and nearer to thy pure and righteous thought. Inspire us with the divine faith, subdue us to the lowly patience, of those who have lived as fellow-workers with thee: and whether thou call us to rejoice in spirit, or to be sorrowful even unto death, may we still abide in thee, and remain without elation and without despair. Remembering that the time is short, and looking to eternal things, may we have one only care, to abate the transitory ill and be faithful to the everlasting good. Day by day may we grow in faith, in self-denial, in charity, in heavenly-mindedness; in the purity by which we may see thee; and the surrender which makes us one with thee. And then, mingle us at last with the mighty host of thy redeemed for evermore. Amen.

MORNING.

ALMIGHTY Father! what are we, that we should stretch forth our hands to thee, and aspire to meet thee, spirit to Spirit? We are less than the least of all thy mercies. We have nothing to bring but thine own gifts, which we have not duly sanctified; and from the shadows of our minds we can but vainly feel after thy light inaccessible. Yet, gracious Lord, though we cannot rise to thee, thy tender mercy bends to us, and draws us with cords of love to own thy secret presence as the soul of every blessing, the solemn look of every duty, the healing anguish of our contrition, and the life of all that is not dead within us. Our help is only from thee: may we keep near to thy refuge, as the shade at our right hand.

Preserve us blameless, O Lord, in our

goings out and comings in this day. Beholding in our hearts the image of thy perfection, may we be pure with a heavenly purity, faithful in our tasks, watchful against temptation, of tender conscience, of patient spirit, of generous temper, and of reverent humility as ever in thy sight. Fill us with the simplicity of a divine purpose, that we may be inwardly at one with thy holy will, and lifted above vain wishes of our own. Help us to keep clean our hearts from unholy thoughts, our lips from rash words, our senses from unworthy indulgence, and our whole life from whatever grieves thy Spirit. Set free from every detaining desire or reluctance, may we heartily surrender all our powers to the work which thou hast given us to do; rejoicing in any toil, and fainting under no hardness that may befall us as good soldiers of Jesus Christ; and counting it as our crown of blessing if we may join the company of thy faithful who have kept thy name and witnessed to thy kingdom in every age. Touch our eyes, O Lord, with clearness, and place the world before them truly; that we may see through its illusions to its sorrows and its sins, and never trust ourselves to it without the shield of faith and the sword of the Spirit, and the unwearied courage of hope and love. Prepare us to seek our rest, not in outward ease, but in inward devotedness: only fulfil unto us the word of the Chief of saints; leave us his peace, while we remain here; and then receive us unto thyself, to mingle with the mighty company of our forerunners. Amen.

MORNING.

GOD of the light,—without, within,—who hast lifted the curtain of night from our abodes! perfect now thy blessing unto us, and take the veil from all our hearts, and make clear unto us the face of thy holy presence. Hide not thyself behind our sinful darkness, gracious Lord! We would not go to do our works alone. Rise with thy morning upon our souls: mingle with the light around us throughout the day; and may we see only as thou showest, and be warmed only with thy glow.

But how, O Lord, shall we abide with thee? What are we, that thou shouldst lay on us the solemn trust of life, and set us a little lower than the angels, and open to us a living communion with thee? We cannot hide even from ourselves our deep unworthiness; and but for thy tender mercy the joy of faith would die within us. For a moment we sigh for thee, but for long days our hearts are cold and dead. For once that the yoke of thy perfect will is our delight, times without number the burden seems too great for our weary affections, and we serve no more. We own all our infirmities and unfaithfulness before thee, O Thou All-merciful. We have nothing to plead, save thine own long-suffering. We must renounce the vain trust in ourselves: but only the more, Thou Strength of the feeble, will we put our trust in thee. O take us out of our own power, by winning our hearts for what thou lovest best, and drawing them into the likeness of thy faithful servants, who have given themselves up to do and to bear all thy perfect will. Redeemed from care by the spirit of sacrifice, may we expect nothing for ourselves, and find our rest in the surrender of all to thee. Our daily work, in solitude or with each other, may we dedicate to thee, who alone art the beginning and the end of whatever is pure and true and holy. And amid the confused voices of the world's sins and sadnesses, may we inwardly hear the whispers of righteousness and hope, and keep clear the vision of thy kingdom. So deepen every better faith within us, that we may be ready to pour some baptism of healing on the doubt and shame and sorrows of other hearts; and may we neither faint nor fail under any grievous cross which thou mayst lay on us. Keep us thine, O Father, in life, in death, and for evermore. Amen.

MORNING.

AGAIN, O Lord of life, we welcome thy holy light, and accept the trust of another day from thee. Thou art the ever-returning dawn to all our darkness: and there is no night, of forgetfulness or sorrow, that turns not back to thee. Sun of our souls, whom we too faintly see! let thy glory break through the clouds of our lower minds, and kindle the fires of pure affection that make us one with thee.

Why art thou ever hid from us, O Father everlasting! Thou art everywhere and fillest all things,—our conscience with thy witness, the hearts of the faithful with thy Spirit, life with thy Providence, and heaven with thy redemption. Yet how seldom do we walk with thee, and move beneath thy searching eye, and feel for the guidance of thy hand! We are ashamed of our sinful blindness, that we discern thee not, and go to think our thoughts and do our works alone. In thy forgiveness be pleased, O Thou Long-suffering, to take the film away, and let in the new life of thy comforting presence. Until we rest in thee, and freely yield our will to thine, there is in us nothing strong and nothing holy; and we do but weary ourselves with chasing the shadows of selfish desire. Wean us, O God, from every secret wish, from every vain expectation, which we dare not spread before thee for thy congenial blessing. And by asking nothing for ourselves and entirely trusting thee, may our yoke become easy and our burden light.

Father of spirits! we bless thee for every gracious and holy soul that hath led us nearer to thee, and especially for him who to us hath chiefly been the way, the truth, and the life. We bless thee that, in every darker passage of our pilgrimage, in the strife of temptation, in the hour of danger, in solitude of spirit, in the weakness of anguish, and the paths of death, we may fix our eye on him as the leader of faithful souls, who hath divinely borne our woes and passed to thy glorious rest. Give us wisdom to walk as he walked; and by keeping ever close to thee may we too have strength to overcome the world. May no pleading of indolence or fear, no levity or vainglory, no coldness of faith and love, withhold us from strenuously doing thy will and finishing thy work.

O Thou who art love and dwellest in love! teach us herein to be followers of thee, as dear children. Never may we shut our hearts against the sorrows of even the unthankful and the evil. Make us organs of thy tender mercy, to soothe the wretched, to lift the penitent, to seek and to save the lost; till all shall at length know themselves thy children, and be one with each other and with thee. Amen.

MORNING.

GOD of our life! Thy loving-kindness is new every morning and thy faithfulness keepeth watch every night. Thou comest to us in every freshness of the light; and even in the darkness it is thy shade that covers us. Our hearts, O Lord, would rise to meet thee, when thou wakenest us to the service of thy will; and sink in trust before thee, when thou leavest us only the shelter of thy rest. Did we remember Thee, O Thou All-patient, as thou rememberest us, our whole life would be as a prayer to thee, and our soul a living sacrifice. O multiply unto us the moments when thou art not lost to our clouded sight, but deeply owned as a fear to our sin, the hope of our aspiring, the stay of our sorrows, and the essence of every holy joy.

O Thou Omniscient! look with pity on

our poverty and emptiness before thee. We know nothing, love nothing, do nothing as we ought. Drawn away from the simplicity of the childlike mind, we wander in mazes where thy truth is not, and turn the face of our pride from the pure shining of thy light. Burdened with the cares of a self-enclosed heart, we often do our work in shameful bonds, and with no free surrender to the calls of gentle affection, and the whispers of thy gracious Spirit. And whenever we go to do our tasks alone, with eye-service and not as unto thee, we grow weary before the time, and no spirit of holy alacrity sustains us. O Merciful Father! we spread our failures and nothingness before thee. In thine infinite plenitude of grace is all that we need : whatever we can desire is eternally present in thee. O deepen the sacred thirst within us, to lead us to thy fountain of life ; and make good the blessed word, "He that asketh receiveth, and he that seeketh shall find, and to him that knocketh it shall be opened."

O Thou whose infinite majesty looketh on us from the heavens and the earth, but whose grace and truth shine in the face of Jesus Christ! more and more soften thy great glory to us through the pure and tender light of his spirit; and enable us to trust thee with his trust, to love thee with his love, to be baptized for life with the baptism that he was baptized with, and drink in death the cup that he drank of. As thou didst dwell in him and bring thy consecration to our humanity, vouchsafe, O Lord, to abide with us, and stay with us till eventide; that we may do all our works as in thy sight, and sweeten our temper with thy constant spirit, and quiet our sorrows with thine inward peace. In the turmoil of the world and the failure of lower hopes, may we remember our real life which is hid with thee; and where our treasure is, there may our heart be also. Keep us by thy mercy in fitness for our change; healing our sins, helping our weakness, sustaining our mortal nature, till we are called to thy higher service. Amen.

MORNING.

O GOD, Thou art our God! early will we seek thee. Our soul thirsteth for thee, Thou Well of life, that springest up eternally! Apart from thee, wandering by our own desires, we never quit the dry and thirsty land, or find the secret refreshment of loving and submissive hearts. Only when we lay open all our weakness in thy solemn presence, and own our inmost sin to thy long-suffering, and renounce our vain reliances for the leadings of thy tender hand, do the clouds of delusion begin to break, and we see from afar the rest that remaineth for thy people. Never, O Thou Spirit of grace! let our sin and heedlessness gather thick upon us: but, day by day, may the way be more clear and the eye more pure for thy blessed light to come.

O Thou all-seeing! we lie before thee in

the shadow of a thousand sins, and are ashamed to speak to thee with our unholy voice. Only on one thing our heart is fixed, —is bent,—that we will trust thee: living or dying, blind or seeing, cast down or lifted up, in the night of weeping or the dawn of joy, we rest upon thy faithfulness and sink deep into thy love. Though we unworthily forget thee, thou never forsakest us, but visitest us with thine awful witnesses of inward dearth and sorrow, till we turn our face to thee and seek our home once more; and thou meetest us on the way and welcomest thy lost that are found again. But O! let nothing even seem to separate us from thine affection. Draw us to the meekness and gentleness of Christ. Reduce us to the childlike mind that is ready for his kingdom and feels for the blessing of his hand. Strip from us the sophistries of self-seeking, of vain custom, of earthly pride and fear; and set free our minds for the reverence of all grace and truth, our hearts for the love of whatever things are pure and good, and our wills for faithful accord with Thine.

O Thou to whom time and eternity are one! where our treasure is, there let our hearts be also. Set our affections on things above, where our real life is hid with thee. Filled with the everlasting light, may we look on each other, and on our work below, and on the strife and sorrows of humanity, with a love and hope that are not of this world. In waiting for the blessed end, may we compose our hearts to a sweet and patient temper, befitting those who are redeemed from self-care by the love of God. Enlarge our souls with a divine charity, that, reviled, we may not revile again; that we may hope all things, believe all things, endure all things; and become messengers of thy healing mercy to the grievances and infirmities of men. In all things attune our hearts to the holiness and harmony of thy kingdom. And hasten the time when that kingdom shall come, and thy will be done on earth as it is in heaven. Amen.

MORNING.

OUR voice shalt thou hear in the morning, O Lord! in the morning will we direct our prayer unto thee and will look up. Not the deepest shade of our ignorance and sin shall withhold our eyes from watching, till thy dawn arise upon our souls. We faint, O Lord, and find no rest, while thou art hid; and all the strength of our unguided steps is weariness and vanity. Never, O Thou Infinite, can our thought avail to reach thee: but thy love is not slow to seek us, and to lead us as a little child that knoweth not how to go out or to come in. O that we may be found of thee, and in all things take thy hand with a loving fear!

O Thou Holiest, whose Spirit bloweth where it listeth! heedless as we are, pass us not by in our unfaithfulness, but speak to us in thy still voice; and as we cover our head and hear, may we hush our idle words, and lay low our guilty pride, and drop every burden of our hearts, that we may be open to thy renewing grace and moulded by thy consecrating will. Amid the outer turmoil of the world thou reservest for us an inner silence of the spirit, where thou wilt ever meet us and give us peace. May the labour of our hands never stop the prayer of our hearts. Cease not to call us to thy secret place: there send the sprinkling of thy dews upon our dry affections; and breathe thou abroad to loose every band of our contracted souls.

O Source of everlasting grace, who hast not left us without thy holy image in our humanity! fill us with the mind that was also in Christ Jesus, who thirsted only to do thy will and finish thy work, and declined no cup of sorrow from thy hand. Fix our eye upon the shadow of the cross which he has left upon every human path, and make us one with him in patience, in pureness, in love, in trust, in divine forgiveness, in entire self-sacrifice. Dying with him to earthly thraldom and mortal fears, may we rise with him to heavenly life and set our affections on things above. Touch us, whilst here, with quickening sympathies, joining us to thy saints and servants of every age; and mingle us, at length, with a more joyful communion, where sin and death shall be no more.

Hear us, O Lord! and let our prayer come before thee as incense, and the lifting up of our hands as the morning sacrifice. And send us thine answer of peace, uniting us in bonds of love with one another and with thee. Amen.

MORNING.

O GOD, our Everliving Refuge! Thou art our shade by night, our light by day; and when we awake, we are still with thee. With grateful hearts we lay at thy feet the folded hours when thou knowest us but we know not thee; and with joy receive from thy hand once more our open task and conscious communion with thy life and thought. For a moment we pause upon the threshold of a new day, and listen for thy voice: for we would not enter, Lord, with unprepared soul, and cannot take a step without thy blessing.

O Fount of wisdom! Light of lights! who knowest every instant more than we could learn in everlasting years! may every opening of truth be to us as a glimpse of thee. Yet let not our deep ignorance be as the hiding of thy face, but only as a call to trust thee, that thou wilt lead the blind by a way that they know not. Whatever else thou mayest withhold from us, O give us purity of heart to see thee, and to trace thy word within our spirits, and follow thy footsteps though they lose us in the mighty deep. As disciples of One who was thy grace and truth in our humanity, and who in his hour of darkness was but closer and dearer to thee, may we abide humbly and reverently with thee; and, in all we think and do and suffer, desire nothing but faithfulness to thy service and nearness to thy love. Bind us to one another, O Thou Holiest, by a common search for thy ways and thirsting for thy Spirit; and raise us to some worthiness of the communion we seek with thy prophets and saints of every age. Day by day liken us more to the spirits of the departed wise and good; and fit us in our generation to carry on their work below till we are ready for more perfect union with them above.

What are we, O Lord, that thou shouldst

make us sharers in thy everlasting work, and give us entrance into thy everlasting rest? It is shameful to think how we have defaced thine image, grieved thy Spirit, quitted thy presence and strayed by ourselves. When we lose thy hand, we are without strength or stay, and sink into the fretful cares and miserable pride of an unloving mind. O call back thy wanderers, gracious Shepherd of our souls, and take us to thy fold again. And if ever we are tempted to forget thee; if our hearts are lifted up in vain security and we know not what spirit we are of, come with thy rebukes, O Lord, and lay them low, till they turn and seek a childlike rest in thee. And if ever we faint under any appointed cross and say "It is too hard to bear," may we look to the steps of the Man of sorrows toiling on to Calvary, and pass freely into thy hand, and become one with him and thee. Let no delusion more come between us and thee. Dedicate us to the joyful service of thy will; and own us as thy children in time and in eternity. Amen.

EVENING.

ETERNAL GOD, for whom no dawn arises and no evening sets, who hast no weary days, no passive hours! again at night-fall we bless thee for giving the rest thou never needest. Thy everlasting work is ever fresh and holy as thine inmost thought: yet hast thou pity on us, whose burden weighs down our mortal strength, and cries out for the wing of immortal power. The failures of this day we lay with sorrow at thy feet. Yet not with faint hearts, not with binding fears, but with a childlike trust, do we cast our weakness on thy strength for a better morrow, and look for thee to lift up thy countenance upon us and show us light. O Thou that bringest deliverance to the captives and songs in the night! scatter our faithless cares to the winds. Humble our self-will beneath the cross. Speak to our conscience with no veil between, till we are wholly at one with thee.

O Source of all perfection! though we are as nothing before thee, except for thy tender mercy, thou art all in all to us,— the dawn to our darkness, the fountain to our thirst, the voice of hope to our sorrows, and the answer of peace to our contrite prayers. Wanderers as we have been, we can bring thee no innocent or untempted hearts, but must still lift up only a penitential cry. But now is it the purpose of our souls to remember thee, and, having chosen the good part which shall not be taken from us, to refer simply to thee all that we think or speak or do. If indeed thou forgivest much to souls that have loved much, thou takest our disquietudes away, and callest us to rest in thee. For thee we long, to thee we cleave, as the secret centre of all good, the hidden sanctity of every blessing and every grief. Touched by thy Spirit, we walk the daily path of life as upon holy ground. No more will our hearts be troubled when that

Spirit,—the only Comforter,—shall abide with us for ever, to be our guide to truth, our source of love, our light of conscience; to wean us from every object of unworthy or excessive desire, from every repining thought, and the fond fancies of mistrustful care. Clear, O Lord, our inward vision, that we may see through the false shows of life, and be kept quiet and true by thy great realities. Waken us all from the dreams of the earthly mind in its forgetfulness of thee. Reveal to the young, O thou Supreme Inspirer, what it is to live this great life of opportunity; and fill them with the pure and undefiled religion which will keep them unspotted from the world. And in the hearts of elders let not the fires die or their work linger, till they are overtaken by the fading light and lengthening shadows of their set time. Knowing nothing of the morrow, may we rejoice to be faithful to-day; gladly accepting the humblest task that waits for us by thy will, and shines with the holy light of thine approval. Amen.

EVENING.

GUARDIAN of our life! look on us in thy compassion, as we bend before thee for thy blessing. Often as we miss thee in the glare and press of day, the shades of evening draw us to seek thee, if peradventure thy countenance may shine upon us in the dark. Not that any search of ours can compass thy perfection: if we stretch our poor wisdom to such heaven of heavens, we are lost alike by noon or night. But unto the meek that only trust thee, thy beauty of holiness ariseth of itself, and from thy presence the cloud removes away. Set our hearts low enough before thee for the opening of thy will; and join us with the contrite whose spirit thou delightest to revive.

O Lord! as we summon the hours of this day to spread their contents before thee, we are conscious how little thine eye can see of any pure order there. The changeful mind that is not stayed upon thee; the vow broken because we trusted in ourselves alone; the selfish desires that shut every window of heaven within us; the anxious cares with which thou hast never burdened us; the temper troubled by flying shadows and lifted into no heavenly calm; all our eagerness of life and fear of death; make for us the shameful confession that our souls are not at one with thee. O Lord! hadst thou forgotten us as we have forgotten thee, we had long ago been as the withered leaf or as the stream of the brook that passeth away. But thou art faithful even to the faithless; and it is thine oldest counsel that thy mercies shall be ever new. We renounce our pride before thee, and lament our bondage to that which we have no right to serve. Bring again our captivity, O Thou great Deliverer! Turn us unto thee, O Lord, and we shall be turned. Renew our hearts with thy pure grace.

Father in heaven, who hast chosen for thy temple the spirits of all faithful men, and wilt be worshipped only in spirit and in truth! henceforth may we do all our work, not seeking our own will, but the Will of Him that sent us. And, lest we too much please ourselves, may we choose some task of faith and love for thy sake alone; and let our patient constancy be the pledge of thy comforting presence. What is weak in us, strengthen by thy grace; gather what is scattered; what is bruised, heal. The help and mercy which we need, may we also be ready to give; having patience with the infirmities of the froward, pity for the sorrows of the afflicted, a free hand for the wants of the friendless, and a hopeful charity for all men. Whenever we faint and fail, remind us of the faithful that have served thee in every age and found in thee their Everlasting Rest. And be thyself also our strong Salvation: for unless thou renew our strength as the eagle, the wing of our wearied soul doth not avail to reach thee.

From hour to hour, from trial to trial, let us but abide simply in thee: and then, though we know not the issue of a day, we will ask no question of the morrow. Only train us for the higher mansions of thy house, where the burden of our days shall be laid down, and the tears of sorrow be wiped away. Amen.

EVENING.

CLEAR in thy sight, Soul-searching God, we now place ourselves at the close of another day, that we may render our account of it to thee: nay rather, that we may learn to see its hours as they lie before thee, who knowest us better than we know ourselves. We do but come to thee at a few set times, going forth on the wings of the morning to meet thy blessing, and returning to thy shelter within the shades of night. But thou abidest ever with us, as a silence behind the voices of the world, the truth within its illusions, and the shame secreted in its sins. Thou tracest our pilgrimage, and no step on its way is hid from thee. O that thou wouldst purify our vision, that we may know even as we are known!

O God, Thou infinite and solemn Presence! if we have not had thee in all our thoughts, it is that we are not pure enough in heart to see thee. We have pleased ourselves instead of serving thee: we have lived in this world without remembering that it is thine. We have fled with coward spirit from the earnest battle of life, and made a shameful peace with our temptations. We have believed rather the flatteries of selfish desire, than the stern voice of duty and the inspiration of pure affection, till truth and goodness float as the unsteady mist before our doubting eye. How often do we delude ourselves with vain shows of good, and spend our passions on the thing that is not! We are like the thirsty who dreameth, and behold, he drinketh; but he awaketh, and behold, he is faint. O Thou whose patience we have too long tried! after so many ineffectual vows, we almost fear to repent, lest we only add one unfaithfulness more, and turn our last strength into weakness.

But, O Thou Eternal! while thou livest, the waters of healing cannot cease to flow; and, feeble as we are, some gracious hand of thy holy ones shall take us to the spring.

O that thou wouldst increase our faith! that we may no longer lean on our broken will, but throw ourselves freely open unto thee, and simply watch thy guiding light, and follow where thou mayst lead. Till we serve thy will with a surrendered heart, we know that thou canst not refresh our weary life, and give us beauty for ashes and the garment of praise for the spirit of heaviness. Accepting the meekness of Christ, may we find each holy truth grow clear, each sacred burden light, and the shadow of guilt dissolve away. Lifted above the mean ambitions of this world, may we live the life of him who, when he was reviled, reviled not again, and dwelt among us as one that served. While we look to be partakers of thine eternity, may we waste no moment of our time, but fill it with the order of a pure mind, a ready love, and an unsparing alacrity. And thus, when the hour strikes for our departure, may we be found worthy to join that higher communion of saints, where sorrowful mysteries are not felt, and the faithful are tried no more. Amen.

EVENING.

PENITENTIAL PRAYER.

O THOU Everlasting God, who fillest immensity! may we indeed lift our eyes unto thee? and wilt thou take account of our low thoughts and trivial cares, which must enter our evening confession? How far must thy tender mercy exceed the awe of thy majesty, that we can stand before thee and live! With but a breath of thy power we are driven to and fro, as a broken leaf before the wind. In the twinkling of an eye thou canst melt the earth into nothing and roll up the heavens as a scroll. Yet do we dwell with thee in perfect peace, and go out and in, as under the secret shadow of the Almighty.

O Lord, if still we seek thee with a heart of hope and yield ourselves to thee, it is that thou ever dealest with us as Sons, though we have not loved and served thee as a Father. Our headstrong wills have not been restrained by thy constant eye, or recalled by thy secret voice to a right and quiet mind. Our tempers have not been gentle and easily entreated, as becometh the children of a forgiving God. Straying from the light of love and duty, our foolish hearts have been darkened, till we know not what spirit we are of. Ah, Lord! our slumbering souls bear witness how we have forgotten thee. If thou hadst been there, our conscience had not died. And even now, may this sleep not be unto death: but visit us with the light of thine arising, that we may awake and see thy glory.

God of grace, whose compassions fail not! Thou wilt look unto the most distant wanderer whose face turneth back to thee. Though we are still a great way off, thou seest that we would arise and go to our Father; and thou wilt welcome thy lost children found again. Henceforth may we serve thee with a willing mind, being never slothful in our task and always fervent in our spirit. If we cannot lift our hands in innocency, may we attain the wisdom of them that see their ignorance, the lowliness of them that sorrow for their pride, the victory of them that surrender all to thee. In our daily course, meet us on the way with warnings of duty, and memories of thy providence, and if needs be, with wrestlings in the night, lest we become estranged from thee. Dispose us, as comrades on the thorny path, to bear one another's burdens; and fill us with that charity which suffereth long and is kind. Sweeten the bitter fountains of our hearts with a branch of that tree of life whose leaves are for the healing of the nations; and may drafts of pure affection refresh us on the desert way. O Thou that passest by and we see thee not! we put our trust in thee. Humble us in the pride of strength; uphold us in the hour of weakness. Make us resolute and true in our days of toil: and in the pauses of rest and sorrow let thy holy angels pitch their tents around us and keep with us the midnight watch. Amen.

MORNING OR EVENING.

ETERNAL GOD, to whose shelter we ever fly! When our thoughts go forth to seek thee, they are lost in such infinitude. Yet, though thy ways are unsearchable, we cannot and would not depart from before thee, but would rest and lie still on thee, to go whithersoever thou wilt till thou callest us home.

Father of spirits! our cry to thee is only for mercy and for help. Teach us to remember our sins with so effectual a sadness that thou, Lord, mayst remember them no more. Mortify within us all vanity and self-will. If our hearts are heated with fires of passion and self-indulgence, oh! cool them with the dews of a heavenly purity. If they are encrusted with worldly desires and shut up in thick cares, be pleased to break us with sorrow and set us free. Teach us, by thy ways of gentleness or of severity, that we are not our own, but thine;—appointed, not to do our own foolish pleasure, but to watch thy directing looks and follow the orders of thine eye. Subdue us, good Lord, to the humility of Christ. For the hardness of pride give us the strength of meekness. Dispose us, in the spirit of a loving child, to take thy hand, though thou leadest us by paths that are dark and strange. May we hold all thy gifts as in trust from thee. Never, by the custom of thy mercies, let us take occasion for complaint and reluctance when they are withdrawn. Though thou only lendest us that which we may love, we bless thee that the love itself thou givest us for ever. And whenever thou rendest our comforts from us, oh! refresh us with the memories of a grateful heart and the hopes of a holy faith.

Disposer of life, who appointest unto all their tasks, and measurest out their days of service! behold, our time is short and our work is great: give us the soul of industry and a heavenly spirit of alacrity, that when the shadows of evening close, we may be able to say "It is finished." As thou workest hitherto, with sleepless mercy, for us, so may we work with thee; and morning and evening find us ready for thy perfect will. May our souls be as one that fulfilleth the night-watches;—awake with a constant awe, and strong with a divine courage; communing with thee in our silent walks of duty, and looking for the light of thy everlasting morning.

O Lord, hear! O Lord, forgive! Save us from our faithless hearts: fortify us to do and to bear thy whole will. When thy storm cometh, shelter us in the clefts of the rock; and lead us forth again under thy peaceful heaven, with souls unharmed. Make us thine through Jesus Christ, O Lord, for ever. Amen.

MORNING OR EVENING.

ETERNAL SPIRIT of our spirits! God of our wonder and our love! Where art Thou, that we may lay our cares to rest in thine infinitude? Thou passest by and we see thee not: yet we turn our eyes to thee more than they that watch for the morning. Thou keepest silence always: yet hast thou opened our ears for thy voice, as of them that listen to the wind. We cannot find thee: yet we cannot leave thee. Our noblest life is rooted and grounded in thee, and we cannot tear ourselves away. If we forget thee, we are as the reed without water, that drieth up and withereth to nought. And yet, O Lord, we *have* forgotten thee: and therefore our nature is poor, our faith is faint, and our hearts are parched up with cares. Still, suffer us not to perish, as cumberers of the ground; but, O Thou Well of life! flow by and give us hope that, at the scent of the living water, our branch may bud and our fruit be multiplied.

O Thou who art and art to be! there are no seasons unto thee. But unto us thou hast appointed a set time upon the earth, and the shadow on our dial lengthens out. Our moments of faithful duty follow us from the past and do not perish: our wasted hours we cannot gather up and they are clean gone for ever. Hasten us, even with thy chastisements, O Thou great Taskmaster, and say unto us, "Fulfil ye your works ere the sun goeth down." Remind us of thy servant Jesus, who in fewest days finished thy divinest work; and fill us with his spirit of holy alacrity. In the loneliness of temptation, may we be steadfast through all the faintness of our soul, and stand in awe and sin not. In the open world, may we take no rest till we have wrought the perfect will of him that sent us. In the retreat of anguish, may we still say, "The cup which my Father hath given me, shall I not drink it?" and rise up to bear our cross with patience. Amid the vain shows of the world and the battle of a godly life may we never be bewildered or dismayed; remembering that the souls of the righteous are in thy hands, and there shall no evil touch them.

O God, Thou watch of our nights and witness of our days! may thy constant presence compose and harmonize our spirits, melting away our fretful cares, consuming our selfish desires, and filling us only with pure and true affections. Soon, O Lord, we shall be spent and gathered unto thee: in the awfulness of so great a lot, let all disquiet cease and the voices of contention be hushed.

Wondrous and eternal God! our life is but a spark that flieth upward in the night. In a moment it is gone, unless thou take us with the righteous to be the lustres of thy firmament, and set us among stars for ever and ever. For time and for eternity we commit ourselves to thee, O Thou God of the living in all worlds. Amen.

MORNING OR EVENING.

O THOU who alone art good! Sole Fountain of life and truth, in whom there is no darkness at all! Thou art a God of awful presence, and besettest our path behind and before. We know that thou seest us, when we are most blind to thee. O Thou piercing light! Thou all-searching Eye! Thou hast entered our inmost souls, that there may be no escape from thee. Now and here, O Lord, we would cast every self-deluding veil away. Behold us as we are; and show us to ourselves, lest we stray into deeper mazes whence thou art hid.

O God most holy! if none but the pure in heart might draw nigh to thee, we could but stand afar, and cry "Depart from us, we are sinful men, O Lord!" In turning our face to thee, we remember how many things thou hast against us: for proud thoughts and idle words and unloving deeds: for wasted moments and reluctant duties and too eager rest; for the vain fancy, the wandering desire, the scornful doubt, the untrustful care; for impatient murmurs and unruly passions and the hardness of a worldly heart;—Thou, Lord, canst call us into judgment, and we have nought to answer thee. But, O most Merciful! the contrite also are dear to thee while the purer fires of their hearts are not yet wholly quenched. And thou art witness that we do not love our guilty ways. O make our conscience true and tender, that we may duly hate them as enemies to thee. Stir up within us an effectual repentance, that we may redeem the time that we have lost, and in the hours that remain may do the work of many days.

Father of spirits, that lovest whom thou chastenest! correct us in our weakness as children of men, that we may love thee in our strength as sons of God. May the same mind be in us that was also in Christ Jesus, that we may never shrink, when our hour comes, from drinking of the cup that he drank of. Wake in us a soul to obey thee, not with the weariness of servile spirits, but with the alacrity of the holy angels. Fill us with a contempt for evil pleasures and unfaithful ease; and sustain us in the strictness of a devoted life. Daily may we crucify every selfish affection, and delight to bear one another's burdens, to uphold each other's faith and charity, being tenderhearted and forgiving as we hope to be forgiven. Hold us to the true humility of the soul that has not yet attained; and may we be moderate in our desires, diligent in our trust, and content with the disposals of thy Providence.

Lord of life and death! Thy counsels are secret: thy wisdom is infinite. We know not what a day may bring forth. When our hour arrives, and the veil between the worlds begins to be lifted, may we freely trust ourselves to thee and say, "Father, into thy hands I commend my spirit." Amen.

MORNING OR EVENING.

O THOU Eternal, in whom is all our trust! again we bring our prayer to thee. But we cannot name thee with a fit and holy Name. Where art Thou, Life of our life, that we may join all wise and blessed souls in serving thee? Thou art too near for our eye to see thee, too far for our labouring mind to reach. Yet art thou ever in the midst: and through all the paths of our lot, and the changes of our hearts, and the numbering of our days, we are alone unchangeably with thee.

Why, then, O Father everpresent, are we so unlike to thee, and quite unworthy to be called thy children? We have wasted the hours thou hast trusted to our care, and served the appetites thou hast given us to rule. We have not learned the heavenly wisdom by which the yoke of life becomes easy and its severest burden light; but are still chafed by restless cares, depressed by light sorrows, and provoked by trivial infirmities. O Lord, thou hast given us souls conscious of holiness and sin: we know our shortcomings: we mourn our slavery: to thee we fly. Quicken us again with thy free Spirit.

O Righteous God! It is a solemn thing to live by day and night beneath thy constant eye and move onwards to thy mysterious eternity. Touch us with a sacred dread, that we may stand in awe and sin not; and then, may we have no other fear. Open our ears, as at a midnight watch, that we may be intent at the faintest approach of evil, and the softest whisper of thy grace. Fill us with thy love of pureness, that we may redeem our lives from confusion, and lift up our wills from weakness, and in our conscience draw nearer to thy peace. Amid the temptations of passion and the eagerness of the world may we be of quiet heart; seeing that the fashion of this world passeth away. Set together by thee on the same field of duty and of danger, may we be all of one heart and mind; in pity relieving, in mercy forgiving, and in honour preferring one another; able to endure hardness together, as true soldiers of the cross; and seeing that we fall not out by the short and narrow way that leadeth unto life.

O God for ever faithful, ever sure! we commit ourselves to thee. There is no place or time where thou art not. Let us not die alone, O Lord! In the shadow of that hour, let thy light arise and shine. And unto thee, who canst keep our souls from death, may we render then the offering of purer praise and the service of immortal powers. Amen.

MORNING OR EVENING.

GOD of all power and might! Thy secret place shall be our shelter still. On one thing our heart is fixed, that we will put our trust in thee, though terrors also are around thee. Thou hangest the world upon nothing: yet we dwell thereon in peace. Thou barest thine arm in the lightning: yet we work in the fields which thou smitest, and own it as the messenger of thy perfect will. Darkness and tempest are often round thee; yet we expect thy light behind every cloud.

But, O God most just! let not our security be the confidence of fools. Never may our blind hearts say "How doth God know? the heavens are covered that he seeth not;" but always may we lie open to thy living presence, and in the silence of the night, when deep sleep falleth upon man, feel the passing of thy Spirit and say "We are not alone, for the Father is with us." Only on thy tender mercy can we rest. When we look up to thee, we dare ask for no recompense for obedience, lest we receive only the wages of sin, and die: but we leave ourselves to thine infinite pity, in the hope that to them that have loved much and repented with many tears, thou wilt say, "Your sins are forgiven; go in peace."

O Thou Guide of the wanderer! our mystic cloud by day and fire by night! though we have erred from thy ways in the desert of our temptation, thou knowest that we have not wholly gone astray. Our secret spirit still searcheth after thee: "As the hart panteth after the water-brooks, so thirsteth our soul after thee, O God." Cool the heats of our passion, refresh the barrenness of our desires, and be to us a wellspring of everlasting life. Visit us with the new birth into the meekness and lowliness of Christ, that we may look not every one on his own things, but every one also on the things of others; emptying our wills of pride, and our hearts of complaining, and laying down all our glories before the cross. Amid the profusion of thy gifts, may we remember that we are disciples of one who had not where to lay his head. Make us ashamed of sloth and indulgence, and ever ready to deny ourselves, and offer ourselves up, a living sacrifice to thee. Let no act, or word, or thought of ours intercept our constant look to thee: and bearing in our conscience a hope of thy peace, may we be at peace. For when thou givest quietness, who, Lord, shall make trouble?

O God of our life! we know not our hour, and thou keepest silent about our end. In a moment we may die, and at midnight be taken away without hand, and be seen no more. May we maintain our watch with patience, and be ready, without any struggling will, to make the lonely pass with thee. Through life and death strengthen us, O Lord, to meet all thy perfect will. Amen.

MORNING OR EVENING.

LORD of all worlds! Thou living God, whom the heaven of heavens cannot contain! We know that thou art with us really, though we forget thee. Thou art in the light, though it alone is visible; and in the darkness, though, when we feel after thee, we cannot find thee. All places are compassed by thine immensity: all times belong to thine eternity. And thy Spirit, which searcheth all things, visiteth our souls, as the wind that bloweth where it listeth, and we cannot tell whence it cometh or whither it goeth: yet it dwelleth with us as the image of a voice. When it divideth for us sacred things from profane, may we veil our head in meekness, and listen to it with a perfect trust.

O Righteous God! Now that we look up to thy pure and awful eye, we discover the hardness of our hearts. Thou hast trusted us in vain with this solemn life. We have abused its opportunities to our poor pleasure, and have trodden with careless feet its sacred ground of duty. In the presence of thy constant pity we have shut our thoughts against mercy and indulged a selfish mind. Amid the refuge of thy Providence, we have been harassed like those that have no God, and shed many faithless tears. And in hearing of thy blessed and inspiring call, we have not hastened to the work which thou hast given us to do, but have been like him who promised with vain lips, saying, "I go, Lord," yet went not. When in the darkness of our transgressions we think of thine infinite holiness, thy voice awakes us like thunder in the dead of night: and we are alone with thy dread power.

Yet, O Thou all-merciful! we dare not be afraid of thee. For thy grace, appearing in all great and holy souls, hath taught us that perfect love which casteth out fear. Nothing but evil trembleth before thee; and our spirits have not wholly gone astray, but look to thee from afar, and turn with longing hope to a diviner life. Rouse us, O Lord, from the sleep of insensibility and the dreams of pleasurable sin. Show us that the precious daylight is far spent; and, while there is yet time, may we finish the task whereunto we are sent.

O Lord Almighty! the soul in anguish, the troubled spirit crieth unto thee. In every sorrow which awaits us, may we look up without despair. If we are driven by strong trouble, as a bird before the storm, may we find shelter in thee, as in the clefts of the everlasting Rock which the tempests cannot shake. In whom should we put our trust but in thee who canst not fail? Times are not hidden from the Almighty; and we would resign ourselves into thy hands for evermore. Amen.

MORNING OR EVENING.

INFINITE GOD, who alone hast always been and changest not! from whom nothing passeth and is gone and to whom no new thing ever can appear! In thee only do we find our unfailing refuge. How can we fix ourselves in thee, that our purposes be not broken off, and we pass not without hope away? For our light is short, pursued by the darkness; and at noontide we are without strength and ready to fade. In thy calmness remember our vain troubles, gracious Lord! And in our doubts and fears may we remember thy constant perfectness. In our blindness and amazement thou art at our right hand with thine infinite realities. And at this very moment thy thought containeth the mysteries we yearn to know, and seeth all the past at which we wonder, and the future in which we trust. As Thou, who knowest all things, art the Everblessed, may we, in the repose of faith, take courage and be glad.

O Sanctifying God! Inspirer of great and saintly souls, who hast given us discernment of the divine trust of life! Fill us with a true and faithful spirit,—ashamed to sleep, while thou lendest light for another duty, resolute to work thy will, till all our strength be spent, prepared for cheerful rest when thou wilt have us wait and be ready to depart. Never, in the crush and storm of life, may we quench thy secret spirit; but so cherish it that, amid earthly and transitory things, it may fill us with the glow of heavenly affections and the light of tranquil faith.

Father of men, who regardest thy children with compassion! Behold this earth, which thou hast given to our care, hath many griefs, and is sad with a weight of shameful sins. Keep us pure from the evil, and make us strong to contend against it. Let us not shut our hearts against pity, O Thou All-merciful! but seek to heal the wounds with which our fellow-men lie stricken on the way. May we make no peace with oppression; but, amid the negligence of the world and the seduction of guilty custom, put into us the spirit of the holy prophets and martyrs of old, that we may cry aloud and spare not. Yet, O Lord, may it be that we sin not in our anger. Touch us with the gentleness of Christ; and so lift up within us a meek aspiring mind, that we may never say to our brother "I am holier than thou," but only ask of thee "God, be merciful to me a sinner!"

So may we labour and watch and pray for the coming of thy kingdom. Amen.

MORNING OR EVENING.

O THOU in whom we live and move and have our being! who hast created and known us, one by one! All generations shall worship thee, while sun and moon endure. Thine we must needs be: if thou but look for us, we are; and if thou but hide thy face, thou prevailest against us, and we pass away. Yet thine alone we fear not to be: for thou wilt have all things ordered well, and none can take us out of thy hand that holds us. Though the heavens should be rolled together as a scroll, and all their host fall down as the leaf falleth from the vine, thou wilt keep the faithful souls that trust thee and there shall no evil touch them.

But, O Most Holy, beside whom there is none good! Why must we ever approach thee as wanderers returning from afar?

Did we keep near thee with a constant mind, and compose our hearts in converse with thee, there were no lot so blest as ours. Yet how often do we remember thee no more! In our idle words, we forget thy listening ear; in our time of wealth, thy watch upon our trust; in the world's vain show, thy great reality; and in our anxious troubles, thy waiting to bear the burden for us. We are ashamed of our sinful delusions, and would guard against them with a more vigilant spirit. O that thou wouldst speak to us in our temptations, show us how vain it is to call evil good, sustain us in our weakness, and suffer not our foot to be moved!

O Thou Everlasting Hope of men! Why should we deem thee a stranger upon the earth, as a wayfarer that tarrieth for a night and turneth aside? Thou art yet in the midst, if we but seek thee with an open soul. May we begin anew to do thy will, that we may know thee as the Living God; renouncing every low desire which may turn the light that is within us to darkness, and surrendering ourselves to that love of what is pure and true, by which we become children of the Highest. In malice, may we be as infants; in understanding, as men; in truth, as the martyrs; in affection, as the angels. May we be fearless to speak, and constant to do, thy perfect will; ready for the earthly cross, or for the heavenly rest; and faithful to take the bitterest cup of duty, that may not pass from us except we drink it.

Father of spirits! We yield ourselves to thee. We will be afraid of neither sorrow nor death in a world where many saintly souls have sanctified them by a divine patience, and amid a Providence wherein no evil thing can dwell. Clinging unto thee, we shall not perish with the fashion of this world that passeth away. As sparks falling on the river, so shall the glories of our strength go out. But the graces of the holy soul shall be as the brightness of the firmament, and as the stars for ever and ever. In thee, O Lord, is our undying trust. Amen.

MORNING OR EVENING,

THE day is thine, O Lord; the night also is thine. In the morning we wait on thee to renew our strength: in the evening, to find the shelter of thy wing. Thou art our Sun; and apart from thee our toil is blind and weary, and there is no glory in our joy. Thou art our Shade; and only when thou closest round us, can our spirits find their rest. Blessed and abiding God! let us not seek thee far, for thou art here; but only lay our hearts low before thee, and thou wilt enter in.

How long have thy servants thirsted after thee, thou spring of everlasting life! In this land of our home the meditations of ages surround us, and through the treasured thoughts of the wise in many generations we are lifted into a light beyond the solitary soul. Countless are thy witnesses,

Eternal God! the stars without number are but a little part of them; and the prayers and aspirings of every heart of man can never cease to speak thee. Humbled and blind amid thy manifold glories, may we find rest in the simplicity of Christ, and be among the pure in heart who alone can see thee. Save us from feeling after thee in vain through the darkness of a selfish and unchastened mind. By thy tender grace shame away all prejudice and scorn, melt down our pride, quiet our fears, sweeten our affections, and lift us above the fretfulness of the world into thy divine repose. And, O Arm of the Lord! awake our slumbering and heedless wills, that we may take all our yoke, and give ourselves up to thee, not by inward vision only, but by faithful service. As Thou, O Father, workest everlastingly, and not one of thy blessings ever faileth, may we never grow weary of well-doing; but still follow the steps of thy beloved Son to-day and to-morrow, till the sacrifice of ourselves be perfected.

O Thou, whose Word hath appeared, full of grace and truth in our humanity, and in the humiliation perfected the holiness of life! more and more let the same mind be in us which was also in Christ Jesus, that we may divest ourselves of every claim, and look for no final peace without the cross. By a patient, loving, trustful spirit, steadfast under evil and hopeful of all good, may we rise into ever nearer communion with thee; and then, in thine own best time, when we are purified by dews of thy grace on our repentance and prepared for the rest that remaineth, join us at length to the august and saintly company of thy redeemed.

Hear our suppliant cry, O Lord; and have regard to it, not by the measure of our deservings, but according to the fulness of thy mercy. Amen.

MORNING OR EVENING.

UNTO Thee, O Source of life and strength, we lift our longing eyes again. Look on us in thy pity, Lord: shine upon us with thy grace: receive us into thine affection. What abiding stay have we in heaven or on earth but thee alone, who art and wast and art to come? To us belong the courses of ceaseless change: we come and go, we live and die, we pass through the light and darkness of this world; and it is not given to us to say "Here will we rest." But around thee, the Centre of all, day and night, summer and winter, joy and sorrow, circle continually, and come not nigh to thee. Wert thou only great in thine infinitude, Most High! the world would be but vanity and our life as nothing before thee. But thy love also is infinite and deemeth nothing small which thou hast made: and our souls, created in thine image and visited by thy Spirit, thou callest to meet thee face to face.

O Thou, on whose goodness we lie down, like the flock upon the green pastures, and from whose purity we quench our thirst, as from the clear waters! many of thy mercies do we plainly see, and we believe in a boundless store behind. No morning stars that sing together can have deeper call than we for grateful joy. Thou hast given us a life of high vocation, and thine own breathing in our hearts interprets for us its sacred opportunities. Thou hast cheered the way with many dear affections and glimpses of solemn beauty and everlasting truth. Not a cloud of sorrow, but thou hast touched with glory: not a dusty atmosphere of care, but thy light shines through! And lest our spirits should fail before thy unattainable perfection, thou hast set us in the train of thy saints who have learned to take up the cross of sacrifice.

O with what glad thanks would we praise

thee, Gracious Lord! did we not know that our thoughtless lives would contradict the song upon our lips! For we have rendered but a cold answer to thy free affection, and have abused our trust to the poor purposes of our own will. Thine awful presence we have forgot. Of thine everlasting law of duty we have made light. Thine immortal promise has but faintly shone upon our sorrows. And our feverish desires have scarcely felt the cool sprinkling from thy well of life. O Lord! how long shall we delude ourselves by the pressure of vain custom, and the flatteries of our idle hearts? Let the time past suffice to have wrought our own will, and now make us consecrate to thine. Whenever we grow eager for unworthy things or troubled about mean cares, turn on us that look of thine which shows us all our littleness and all thy deep compassion. Let thy Spirit be felt to hover near our souls: and beneath the air of its wing may every passion lie quiet, and all our better love spring up with hope and power. In care, in haste, in provocation, keep us ever even, ever still. In temptation, make us quick and clear and strong. Amid threats and evil opinion give us a prophet's heart to disregard the favour of men and simply heed the truth of God. And in all our passage through this world of many sins and sorrows, fill us with Christ's own patient and helpful spirit, open to every holy affection, and always ready to comfort and forgive. Thus own us, Heavenly Father, as thy true children, and prepare us for thy more intimate presence. Amen.

MORNING OR EVENING.

O GOD, our Father! Spirit of Grace and goodness! Thou dwellest with the souls that will dwell with thee, and comest forth to meet us when we seek thee truly. Art thou not here, O Lord, and in thy servants' silent hearts, waiting for their thoughts of penitence and prayer? Hast thou not said "Seek ye my face?" Thy face, Lord, will we seek. Lo! we come to learn thy perfect will.

Without thee, O Lord, we cannot live; for thou art our only light: and without thee we dare not die; for thou art our life when we seem to perish. Amid all our changes, thou canst not fail. Unto thee all things are of old, from everlasting days: but unto us who are of yesterday thou hast made all things new. We are as strangers in thy wondrous universe: yet as children at home within thy shelter, thou dear and blessed God.

O Father, who grantest nothing to our complaints, but thy best blessings to our love and trust! inspire us with an entire and joyful confidence in thee. May we learn to forget our own poor will in seeking and in bearing thine. We know, O Lord, that we cannot understand thy Providence: for we and all that we behold are in its awful stream, and there is nothing fixed but thee. In thy hands are all our hearts and ways, as the rivers of water, to turn them whithersoever thou wilt. The courses of our lot we leave to thee. Only, whether thou take them through the rocky desert or by the green pastures, make them to overflow with the waters of life, and replenish them from the fountains of thy holy hill.

O Thou Strength of the righteous! Inspirer of the true Seers and Prophets, and chiefly of the Man of Sorrows whose spirit was no other than thine own! how tender is thy mercy, if it is like His who was grieved in our griefs, and rejoiced to bear our sicknesses away! how awful thy rebukes, if they smite, like his, upon the heart of sin! how healing thine approval, which seeth, like his, in secret, and blesseth the mite of a pure charity, and calleth to itself the hearts in which there is no guile! The lowly who had feared thee are glad, O Lord, that Thou, incomprehensible in thine infinitude, standest revealed in thy holiest servants whom we may approach and love; and that in following them we may best resemble thee. May the sanctity of their faith and spirit rest upon all our life, refreshing the weariest task and making our daily toil divine; teaching us not to be pleasers of ourselves, but to restrain our wayward will and desire that only which is right; filling us with shame for our great shortcomings and a patient striving after a better mind; possessing us with such pity and labour for the ills of men as may lead us towards the peace of God; and strengthening us to sow the field of duty even in weeping and in fear, that others may reap hereafter the fruits of joy and love.

Dwell closely with us while we live, O Lord, and stay with us when we die,—the steadfast light of our hearts, and our portion for ever! Amen.

MORNING OR EVENING.

O GOD, Thou only Refuge of thy children! who remainest true though all else should fail, and livest though all things di Cover us now when we fly to thee. Thy shelter was around our fathers. Thy voice called them away, and bids us seek thee here till we depart to be with them. In thy memory are the lives of all men from of old. Before thy sight are the secret hearts of all the living. We stand in awe of thy justice which, since the ages began, hath never changed: and we cling to thy mercy that passeth not away.

Lord of life! we cannot go where thou and thy blessings are not spread abroad. Nothing is deep and high as thou, whose spirit dwelleth in the roots of the ocean and is clothed with the foldings of the heavenly light. In secret thou fillest the earth and sky and all things that are known by the seeing of the eye and the hearing of the ear: but thou art open only to the cleansed heart. We know that of thine excellency we cannot fitly speak; though it be the constant wonder of our minds. But, O Lord, it is only because our souls are dull and cold and our tongues are stiff to praise thee.

Almighty Father! Thou art a God afar off as well as nigh at hand. Thou who in times past didst pity the prayers of our forerunners, and especially of that suffering servant of thine whom thou hast made our Leader unto thee! be pleased to strengthen us now, O Lord, to bear our lighter cross and surrender ourselves for duty and for trial unto thee. Show us something of the blessed peace with which they now look back on their days of strong crying and tears, and teach us that it is far better to die in thy service than to live for our own. Rebuke within us all immoderate desires, all unquiet temper, all presumptuous expectations, al ignoble self-indulgence: and feeling on us the embrace of thy Fatherly hand, may we meekly and with courage go into the darkest ways of our pilgrimage; anxious not to change thy perfect will, but only to do and bear it worthily. If the crosses of life must sometimes make us sad, never, O Lord, may they make us ashamed: but may thy wisdom subdue us and thy peace be with us; and when we are weakest, make us strongest. Knowing ourselves, and that in forgetting thee is our greatest infirmity, in cleaving to thee our true dignity and power, may we not be high-minded, but fear. May our aspirations more and more be holy and heavenward. Cool within us all heats of passion: and may thy mercies not fall as snow upon a burning land, but be treasured in the clefts and lie gently on the heights of our soul, and show forth the everlasting sunshine of thy grace. May we spend all our days as in thy presence, and meet our death in the strength of thy promise, and pass thence into the nearer light of thy knowledge and thy love. Amen.

MORNING OR EVENING.

O THOU whose glory filleth all things! whose greatness we can never find, but whose presence we would always seek! whose excellency is more than we can know, yet all that we adore! from the confused voices of our life we turn to thy silent presence: from our dark and bounded sky we issue forth into thy pure and infinite light. O, come, Thou Holy Spirit, we beseech thee! and even to our dull clay bring thy sanctity and dwell.

O God! in time past we have not known thee. Else, how could we ever murmur while thy Providence rules us or neglect any task which thy law of Duty brings? Lord! we believe: Help thou our unbelief! For we have not faith which worketh by love and fainteth not. Our deepest desire is still unto thee. But we are weary to think of our fruitless lives, of the rashness of our self-will and the cowardice of our right affections, of our pride in that which perisheth and our slight of things that are eternal. O for a true heart of trust, to offer ourselves up as a living sacrifice! For what are poverty or riches, affliction or gladness, life or death, to them that have thy constant peace, O Lord?

O Thou, whom all the contrite bless and only the pure in heart can truly know! Fill us with the strength of them that know their weakness, and lean ever upon thee. May the sorrows of our repentance never be unavailing, but lead us to a holy hope, a meek faith, a never-ceasing charity. Expecting nothing for ourselves and utterly trusting thee, may we be ready to suffer any peril or tribulation that may threaten to hinder our duty and make us ashamed. That we are thy children, made partakers of thy spirit, and thine immortality, may we feel to be supreme among our blessings and greater than all our griefs. As thy ceaseless mercies descend upon our hearts, O may they not fall as dews upon the barren rock, but as the small rain upon the herbage that maketh the pastures glad. And when thy cloud encompasseth us and thy mystery maketh us afraid, may we be still, while thou ordainest darkness; and then use thy returning light in more earnest duty and more cheerful love.

O Spirit of grace, who withholdest thy blessing from none! take from us the tediousness and anxiety of a selfish mind, the unfruitfulness of cold affections, the weakness of an inconstant will. With the simplicity of a great purpose, the quiet of a meek temper, and the power of a well-ordered soul, may we pass through the toils and watches of our pilgrimage; grateful for all that may render the burden of duty light; and even in strong trouble rejoicing to be deemed worthy of the severer service of thy will. Amen.

MORNING OR EVENING.

O GOD! Thou Spirit of our secret life, apart from whom our nature faints! weary of ourselves, we come to thy shelter. Our span of troubled days we bring to thy calm eternity. Over our path of pilgrimage we feel the spaces of thy immensity: on the dimness of our pure desires we seek the glow of thy paternal smile: in the strife of sin and the sadness of mortality we find a spirit of power and hope in the memory of thy holy Providence.

Infinite Ruler of creation, whose Spirit dwells in every world! we look not into the solemn heavens for thee, though thou art there: we search not in the ocean for thy presence, though it murmurs with thy voice: we wait not for the wings of the wind to bring thee nigh, though they are thy messengers: for thou art in our hearts, O

God, and makest thine abode in the deep places of our thought and love; and into each gentle affection, each contrite sorrow, each higher aspiration we would retire to meet and worship thee.

Lord of our living conscience, who speakest to us in the voice of duty and pleadest with us in the grief of sin! Thy creatures that know thee not have more truly served thee than our conscious minds; and while seasons and waves obey thy word, our vacillating desires forget to finish thy work, our restless passions keep not the order of thy will. O God! Thou knowest the soul within us, that it is not built up as a sanctuary for thy praise; but is a wreck of broken purposes and fallen aspirations and desecrated affections. Fountain of purity and peace! shed on us the influence of a new hope and holier sympathies: refresh our dry souls with the dews of a true penitence. O that our strength might no more fail, or our wills be deluded, when we strive against the weight of indolence, the seductions of self-love, and the weakness of a desponding mind!

O Father, who dost bless us always even in our griefs, and love us even in our sins! from the spirit of Jesus the crucified whose cry went up unto thee, from his meek triumph, his passage to immortal rest, we would learn to trust thee and look up amid the sadness of thy Providence. O may our affections be more and more followers of thee, as dear children, and spread, like thy tranquillizing presence, wherever suffering is laid low, or the sigh of the oppressed is heard, or remorse retires to weep. May we consecrate ourselves and imitate thee by blessing others. By the breath of a divine love within us may the cloud of anxiety and the storm of fretful passions be swept away. Beneath the light of thy peace may even the valley of the shadow of death be to our feet as the green pastures and the still waters. And when we pass into that land which no eye hath seen, may we be of ready heart to meet our forerunners there, and bless thee that the days of sorrow and temptation are finished. Amen.

MORNING OR EVENING.

O LORD our God, whose eye searcheth for truth and purity of heart! Turn us now away from every vanity of thought, and draw forth some living light of trust and love, that we may meet thee, spirit to Spirit, the weak to the Almighty, the sad and sinful to the only Blessed and Holy. O thou wellspring of eternal life! we bring to thee the thirst we cannot quench: send the cooling drops which shall abate the fever of vain desire and baptize us into peace with thee.

O Thou Everpresent! there is no faithfulness gentle and long-suffering as thine. All our unrest of soul cometh only hence, that we keep not close to thee, nor lay ourselves freely open to thy ready help. Thy calmness is ever by to swallow up our fretful cares; thy silent looks, to chide our eager words; thy infinite purity, to put to shame whatever is mean and low. Every hour of eternity is full of thee. There is no desert place in life or death where thou art not. It is we alone, O Lord, that stray and change: and when our faithless spirits would return to thee again, thou stretchest forth thy hand and comfortest us. Never may we forget thee till sin hath made thee terrible. Hold not thy peace too long with us, O Thou All-merciful! but chasten us betimes, ere we have ceased to lay thy will to heart.

O Thou Eternal, in whose appointment our life standeth! Thou hast committed our work to us, and we would commit our cares to Thee. May we feel that we are not our own, and that thou wilt heed our wants, while we are intent upon thy will. May we never dwell carelessly or say in our hearts "I am here and there is none over me;" nor anxiously, as though our path were hid; but with a mind simply fixed upon our trust, and choosing nothing but the dispositions of thy Providence. Before thee, O Lord, we have no rights, save to serve thee with our toil and love thee in our souls. Yet often have we coveted our rest before the time, and stretched forth our hand to gather it as the hasty fruit before the summer; and so it has been small and bitter to the taste. Henceforth, we would wait upon thy seasons, and leave ourselves to thee. More and more fill us with that pity for others' troubles which comes from forgetfulness of our own; with the charity of them that know their own unworthiness; with the alacrity of mortals that may not boast of the morrow; and the glad hope of the children of eternity. Lead us in the straight paths of simplicity and sanctity; and may neither the flatteries nor the censures of men betray us into a devious step. And when the last dimness steals upon our eyes and draws the veil to hide all earthly light, give us to see in the spirit the gracious angels of thy mercy to bear us from the scenes of time, and feel a spring of joys permanent as the numbers of eternity. And unto thee, the beginning and the end, Lord of the living, refuge of the dying, be thanks and praise for ever! Amen.

MORNING OR EVENING.

PENITENTIAL PRAYER.

O GOD, who art and wast and art to come! who settest forth our years from thine eternity and shapest the heavens from thine immensity! most deeply hidden from us, yet most surely present with us! how can we find thee in our darkness here, seeing that thou holdest back the face of thy throne and spreadest thy cloud upon it? Yet, Lord, all things are possible to thee: Thou canst turn the shadow of death into morning. Though there is nothing clean in thy sight, and thou beholdest the moon and it shineth not, and chargest the angels with folly, yet unto this man wilt thou look, even unto him that is of a humble spirit, and that crieth to thee with a contrite voice.

And how else, O our Witness and our

Judge, can we bring to thee the memory of our unworthiness and the sadness of our confessions? For we cannot wash our hands in innocency, or present the holy hearts in which thou delightest to dwell. Make clear unto us, O Lord, the countenance of thy love, for our sins are heavy upon us. We have not offered unto thee the living sacrifice of our bodies and our spirits, which are thine; but have served the vain imaginations of an unsanctified mind. Living without thee, we have chafed against the ills thou sendest for our patience, and fainted beneath the burden for which thou givest strength, and fallen from the love that burns within us when we gaze on thee. O God of mercy! we have lost the shield of faith and lie before thee stricken by the darts of sin. Heal us with a restoring sorrow, and be with us that we fall no more.

Spirit of spirits! Light of lights! who livest in all great and holy souls, and shinest for us in the face of Jesus Christ! humble us with his lowly surrender unto thee, and incline us, with the simplicity of disciples sitting at his feet, to that good part which shall not be taken from us. Never may we turn our ear from the still small voice in which thou art heard in the deep places of our souls: and, as we listen to it, may the noise of our passions be quieted, and the voice of the charmer be unheeded, and our whole life and death become as an answer to thy call "Yea, Lord, here I am." May we decline no duty which thou sendest; fear no trial which thou appointest, grow cold in no affection which thou approvest. Fill us with all meekness and gentleness; with forbearance to the weak, lest we also be tempted; with pity for the suffering, seeing that we too dwell in houses of clay; with courage against temptation, since thou art on our side; with a spirit of praise and love amid our joys, remembering that we can receive nothing except it be given us of heaven; and with a blessed hope in death, befitting those whose life is hid with Christ in God. Amen.

MORNING OR EVENING.

FIRST ASSEMBLING AFTER DEATH OF A HEAD OF THE FAMILY.

O GOD of light eternal! we look to thee. And though thy cloud is round about thee and the shadow lies upon us here, we know that thy mercy is undimmed; and with perfect trust we wait for thee, as they whose eyes watch for the morning. We own thee as the only Lord of life and death. Do with us as thou wilt: call us to our work, or to our rest: bid us take our burden, or lay it down. We murmur not, O Lord. Only abide with us by night and day; and be our strength to do and bear thy perfect will.

Thou hast sent among us thy sad messenger, O our God, and taken from us thy faithful servant, the leader of our way, to whom our eyes looked up, with whom we took sweet counsel, and whose spirit turned our duties into love. But the sorrow of our hearts pleads with us to bless thee for the sacred ties which thou hast severed, for the holy wisdom, the tender patience, the pure humanity, which have held our spirits in reverence. Thou hast withdrawn them into thy mystic shadows: Thy will be done. Only, take not *all* away: by the image in our souls, leave us whatever has been sweet and strong and sacred in the presence which here we shall know no more; that the voice we have loved may yet reach us through the solemn silence.

O God, Thou Helper of the helpless! look upon this sorrowing home with thy tender mercy. Sustain and comfort every mourning heart. In thy holy keeping are the living and the dead: and all are safe, till thou bring them to thine everlasting light. Give us strength to return to the quiet duties of our place. With chastened desires, with better aspirations, with truer diligence, with less trust in ourselves and more rest in thee; may we dedicate ourselves anew to the service of thy will; that, in the faith and spirit of him who was made perfect through suffering, each of us may be ready to say, whenever the hour shall strike, 'Father, I have finished the work which thou gavest me to do.' Amen.

FOR THE OPENING OF A NEW PLACE OF WORSHIP.

O THOU who alone hast ever been and wilt ever be! Thou appointest to us a beginning of days and end of years which thou knowest not; and wilt not cast away the offerings of our changeful life, or withhold thy consecration from our growing needs and fresher pieties; while still our ancient prayer, seeking only what our fathers sought, is not wearisome to thee. O patient Spirit of Eternity! with what long-suffering dost thou permit the cry of trouble and aspiration unto thee! Thy thought, so solemn in the stars, so beautiful upon the earth, is holy in our souls, and tender in the face of Christ. When we would hide ourselves from thy mystery, we are drawn forwards by thy grace: and when we shirnk away, because we have nothing to render, thou callest unto us 'Give me your heart.'

Our hearts, Lord, would we give, and bring their purest fires to burn upon thine altar here. Yet can we find no incense pleasing to thee because true to us, save the breathing of a contrite spirit: for here beneath thine eye we remember our broken vows, our languid will, our cold affections, and all the disorder of our souls. Lord, thou knowest all things, and not a thought of our mind is hid from thee. Are we not weary of our shortcomings, and, when we see ourselves as thou seest us, do we not abhor our sins? Yea, Lord, our spirit thirsteth for thee, as the traveller faints in the desert for the meadow land and the living waters. Restore the brightness of thy first rising, and let not thy dawn go back and become sad with clouds. Clear the dim eye of our faith, and shine with thy presence on the path before our feet, and sustain us to work while it is yet day; that we may never say 'The daylight is past, the evening is come, and we are not saved!'

O Lord of every world, before whom stand

the spirits of the living and the dead! Thousands praise thee with a voice from which mortal sadness hath passed away. Prepare us to follow their upward track and join their glorious hymn. And while we watch yet one hour here, whether in the retreats of sorrow or on the mount of vision, may we feel the great communion of the faithful of all ages gathered round our souls. And hence may we carry a fresh sanctity and order into our homes; modest desires and pure integrity into the world; forbearance to the wayward; help to the weak; pity to the burdened and afflicted; hope to the fearful; and charity to all men.

Thou art the God of future years. We leave them, with their treasures and their secrets, at thy feet. When our time is past, may our children serve thee with higher faith and nobler hearts. And so long as a generation shall seek thee here, may the careless be awakened, the faithful confirmed, the mourner comforted, and the pure in heart be brought to see their God. May age be filled with cheerful hope, and the hand of Christ shed its blessing on the child. Hear us in thy mercy, O Father Everlasting; and bid thy glory dwell among us, while a heart remains to be filled with love and joy and peace. Amen.

PUBLIC SERVICE OF PRAYER.

MORNING OR EVENING.

¶ *The Minister, entering the desk, and the People, standing, shall say:*

Minister. The Lord be with you.

People. And with thy spirit.

Minister. Come, let us return unto the Lord; and he will raise us up, and we shall live in his sight.

People. Blessed be the Lord God, who turneth not our prayer away, nor his mercy from us.

Minister. The most High dwelleth not in temples made with hands.

People. He is not far from any one of us.

¶ *Then shall the Minister say:*

DEARLY beloved brethren, the heavenly Father in whose presence we now stand is always more ready to hear than we to pray: nor does anything hide him from us but the veil of our impure and earthly mind. And since the preparations of even the willing heart are not without him, let us inwardly pray for the grace of a humble and holy spirit: that for a little while we may be alone with him; and, as his beloved Son went up into the mountain to pray, so we may rise above the haste and press of life, and commune with him in spirit and in truth.

¶ *After a few moments of silence for inward prayer, the Minister shall say the following Prayer; all kneeling, and the People responding with '*Amen.*'*

O GOD, who art, and wast, and art to come, before whose face the generations rise and pass away; age after age the living seek thee, and find that of thy faithfulness there is no end. Our fathers in their pilgrimage walked by thy guidance, and rested on thy compassion: still to their children be thou the cloud by day, the fire by night. Where but in thee have we a covert from the storm or shadow from the heat of life? In our manifold temptations, thou alone knowest and art ever nigh : in sorrow, thy pity revives the fainting soul : in our prosperity and ease, it is thy Spirit only that can wean us from our pride and keep us low. O Thou sole Source of peace and righteousness ! take now the veil from every heart; and join us in one communion with thy prophets and saints who have trusted in thee, and were not ashamed. Not of our worthiness, but of thy tender mercy, hear our prayer. *Amen.*

¶ *Then the Lord's Prayer, to be said by the People after the Minister.*

OUR Father who art in heaven, Hallowed be thy name. Thy kingdom come. Thy will be done on earth, as it is in heaven. Give us this day our daily bread. And forgive us our trespasses, as we forgive them that trespass against us. And lead us not into temptation; but deliver us from evil: For thine is the kingdom, and the power, and the glory, for ever and ever. Amen.

¶ *Then shall be said or sung the following Hymn, called* TE DEUM LAUDAMUS ; *all standing.*

WE praise thee, O God : we acknowledge thee to be the Lord.

All the earth doth worship thee : the Father everlasting.

To thee all Angels cry aloud : the Heavens, and all the Powers therein.

To thee Cherubim and Seraphim : continually do cry,

Holy, Holy, Holy : Lord God of hosts ;

Heaven and Earth are full : of the Majesty of thy Glory.

The glorious company of the Apostles : praise thee.

The goodly fellowship of the Prophets : praise thee.

The noble army of Martyrs : praise thee.

The holy Church throughout all the world : doth acknowledge thee,

The Father : of an infinite Majesty ;

Thy beloved, true : and glorified Son,

Who leadeth us to victory: over Sin and Death;

Thy Holy Spirit also: the Comforter,

Which maketh us sons: by the Spirit of adoption.

We therefore pray thee, help thy servants: whom thou hast redeemed in thy boundless love.

Make them to be numbered with thy saints: in glory everlasting.

O Lord, save thy people, and bless thy heritage: govern them, and lift them up for ever.

Day by day we magnify thee: and we worship thy name ever, world without end.

Vouchsafe, O Lord: to keep us this day without sin.

O Lord, have mercy upon us: have mercy upon us.

O Lord, let thy mercy lighten upon us: as our trust is in thee.

O Lord, in thee have I trusted: let me never be confounded.

¶ *Or the following Canticle:*

MARVELLOUS things of the Lord our God : have we heard and our fathers have told us.

Repeat to their children his ancient praise : that the generations may set their hope in God.

They that trust in the Lord shall be as his holy hill : which cannot be removed;

As the mountains are round about Jerusalem : so the Lord encompasseth them for ever.

The secret of the Lord is with them that fear him : in the time of trouble he hideth them in his pavilion.

In the day-time he leadeth them with a cloud : and in the night with a light of fire.

Though they fall, they shall not be utterly cast down : for the Lord upholdeth them with his arm.

They shall not be afraid of evil tidings : for their times are in his hands.

Because their heart is not haughty, nor their eyes lofty : and they are quiet as a weaned child;

Therefore he lifteth them up : and girdeth them with might, though they know it not.

Commit thy way unto the Lord, wait patiently for him : and thou shalt never be forsaken;

He will draw thee out of the dark waters : and show thee the path of life.

Who is among you that feareth the Lord : yet walketh in darkness and hath no light?

Let him surely trust in the Lord : and stay upon his God.

Lift up your eyes to the heavens : and look upon the earth beneath;

The heavens shall vanish away like smoke : and the earth shall wax old like a garment;

And they that dwell therein : shall die in like manner;

But the salvation of the Lord shall be for ever : and his righteousness shall not fail.

To the Only Holy, the First and the Last : be thanksgiving and praise;

From all kindreds and tongues on earth : and the voices of saints in heaven. Amen.

¶ *Then shall be read the* FIRST LESSON, *taken out of the Old Testament.*

¶ *After that, shall be said or sung the following Canticle:*

SEEK ye the word of the Lord and read: his thoughts are not as our thoughts.

Strengthen ye the weak hands: and confirm the feeble knees;

Say to them that are of fearful heart: Be strong; fear not;

Behold your God will bring deliverance: he will come and save you.

Then shall the eyes of the blind be opened: and the ears of the deaf shall be unstopped.

Then shall the lame leap as the hart: and the tongue of the dumb shall sing.

In the wilderness shall waters break out: and streams in a thirsty land;

The solitary place shall be glad: and the desert shall blossom as the rose.

And a highway shall be there: the way of holiness;

To the meek it shall be a path of light: and the wayfaring man shall not err therein.

Come, walk in his word: with songs of joy;

And sorrow and sighing: shall flee away.

Glory be to God most High: the ever-blessed Father;

Who is, and was, and shall be: world without end. Amen.

¶ *Or the following Canticle:*

GLORIOUS things of thee are spoken: Jerusalem, city of our God.

Of thee it shall be said, Here were the prophets born: here the most High was known;

Look on the mountain of his holiness: a light and joy to the whole earth;

Mark well her towers, and consider her bulwarks: that ye may tell it to generations to come.

O Zion, that bringest good tidings: lift up thy voice to every age;

Let the watchmen cry from thy palaces: 'Behold your God!'

As a banner from thy walls, an ensign from afar: is the testimony of Israel.

For darkness covered the earth: and gross darkness the people;

But the Lord arose as a light upon thee: and his glory was seen upon thee;

Till the Gentiles came to thy light: and thy walls were called Salvation, and thy gates Praise.

We will remember the days of old: the years of the right-hand of the most High;

We will meditate on all his work: and write his law upon our hearts.

O Lord, thou art a God that doest wonders: thou hast declared thyself among the people.

Thy way is in the sanctuary: who is so great a God as our God?

Glory be to God most High: the ever-blessed Father;

Who is, and was, and shall be: world without end. Amen.

¶ *Then shall be read the* SECOND LESSON, *taken out of the New Testament.*

¶ *After that, shall be said or sung the following Canticle:*

SING no more the song of Moses : lift on high the song of the Lamb ;

For the former things have passed away : and heaven and earth have become new.

O Jerusalem, Jerusalem : thy children refused to be gathered ;

But a Zion of heavenly pattern descends : whose builder and maker is God.

The tabernacle of God is with men : he dwelleth not in temples made with hands.

The temple of our holy Jerusalem : are the Lord God himself and the Lamb ;

They are the light that lighten it : though sun and moon should fail.

All day its gates are open : and no night shuts the way of mercy.

Come to the river of God in the midst : to him that is athirst he giveth of its living waters freely.

Come to the tree of life: whose leaves are for the healing of the nations.

Blessed be the Lord that draweth nigh: and openeth deep things of the Spirit to them that love him;

And calleth the kingdoms of this world: to be the kingdoms of our God and of his Christ.

Now unto the God of grace: for the might of his Spirit and the love of Christ;

Be glory in the Church throughout all ages: world without end. Amen.

¶ Then the Minister shall say the following Prayers; all kneeling, and the People responding with AMEN.'

HOLY Lord God; how can we lift up our face, and make mention of thy lovingkindness? for thy praise is only our abasement, and the greatness of thy mercy is the measure of our guilt. Yet turn us not back from thy presence. Look upon us according to our deep need, not our poor deservings. Lift off the burden of our many sins, and revive the contrite that fly to thee. When thou art nigh, we are weary of our selfish desires, our faithless cares, our unresisted temptations : wasted moments, and bitter words, and vain ambitions rise up in judgment against us: we lay at thy feet with shame the vows we have not kept, and the sorrows we have not sanctified. No secret thing is hid from thee./Thou knowest the spirit we are of. Chasten us with thy rebuke, seek us with thy pity, recall us by thy grace, ere we are quite estranged from thee. Let the saving word, once heard on earth, be renewed from heaven, ' Your sins are forgiven ; go in peace.' *Amen.*

O GOD, our everlasting hope, who holdest us in life, and orderest our lot ; we ask not for any prosperity that would tempt us to forget thee. As disciples of one who had not where to lay his head, may we freely welcome the toils and sufferings of our humanity, and seek only strength to glorify the cross thou layest on us. Every work of our hand may we do unto thee; in every trouble, trace some lights of thine; and let no blessing fall on dry and thankless hearts. Redeeming the time, may we fill every waking hour with faithful duty and well-ordered affections, as the sacrifice which thou hast provided. Strip us, O Lord, of every proud thought; fill us with patient tenderness for others, seeing that we also are in the same case before thee; and make us ready to help, and quick to forgive. And then, fix every grace, compose every fear, by a steady trust in thine eternal realities, behind the changes of time and the delusions of men. Thou art our Rock: we rest on thee. *Amen.*

O GOD, thou hast set us in the train of many martyrs and holy men; and given us, as author and finisher of our faith, one who offered himself up a living and dying sacrifice. We are not our own, but thine.

Freely may we crucify our shrinking will, surrender ourselves to the uttermost claims of thy Spirit, and seek no peace but in harmony with thee.

¶ *In response to this the People shall say:*

According to that gracious word, 'Peace I leave with you; my peace I give unto you; not as the world giveth, give I unto you.'

¶ *In Quires and Places where they sing, here may follow an Anthem or Hymn.*

¶ *Then the following Prayers and Intercessions:*

ALMIGHTY Lord, of whose righteous will all things are, and were created; who liftest the islands out of the deep, and preparest not in vain the habitable world; thou hast gathered our people into a great nation, and sent them to sow beside all waters, and multiply sure dwellings on the earth. Deepen the root of our life in everlasting righteousness; and let not the crown of our pride be as a fading flower. Make us equal to our high trusts; reverent in the use of freedom, just in the exercise of power, generous in the protection of weakness. With all thy blessings bless thy servant ~~Victoria~~, our ~~Queen~~; with all the members of the Royal House. (Fill ~~her~~ heart and theirs with such loyalty to thee, that her people may be exalted by their loyalty to her.) To our Legislators and Counsellors give insight and faithfulness, that our laws may clearly speak the right, and our Judges purely interpret it. Let it be known among us how thou hatest robbery for burnt-offering; that the gains of industry may be all upright, and the use of wealth considerate. May wisdom and knowledge be the stability of our times: and our deepest trust be in thee, the Lord of nations and the King of kings. *Amen.*

O THOU whose eye is over all the children of men, and who hast called them, by thy Prince of Peace, into a kingdom not of this world; send forth his spirit speedily into the dark places of our guilt and woe, and arm it with the piercing power of thy grace. May it reach the heart of every oppressor, and make arrogancy dumb before thee. Let it still the noise of our strife and the tumult of the people; put to shame the false idols of every mind; carry faith to the doubting, hope to the fearful, strength to the weak, light to the mourner; and more and more increase the pure in heart who see their God. Commit thy word, O Lord, to the lips of faithful men, or the free winds of thine invisible Providence; that soon the knowledge of thee may cover the earth, as the waters cover the channels of the deep. And so let thy kingdom come, and thy will be done, on earth as it is in heaven. *Amen.*

May the God of all grace, who hath called you unto himself in Christ, perfect, establish, strengthen you: and to him be the glory for ever. *Amen.*

Or

NOW the Lord of peace himself give you peace always by all means. The Lord be with you all. *Amen.* 2 *Thess.* iii. 16.

PUBLIC SERVICE OF PRAYER.

MORNING OR EVENING.

¶ *The Minister shall say one or more of the following sentences, and then the address which comes after; all standing.*

THE way of man is not in himself alone : it is not in man that walketh to direct his steps. *Jer.* x. 23.

Thoughts of peace, saith the Lord, do I think towards you : ye shall go and pray unto me, and I will hearken to you : ye shall seek me, and find me when ye shall search for me with your whole heart. *Jer.* xxix. 11–13.

Give glory to the Lord your God, before he cause darkness, and before your feet shall stumble on the dark mountain, and, while ye are looking for light, he turn it into the shadow of death. *Jer.* xiii. 16.

Let us search and try our ways, and turn unto the Lord: let us lift up our heart with our hands unto God in the heavens. *Lam.* iii. 40, 41.

Know ye not that ye are the temple of God, and that the Spirit of God dwelleth in you? 1 *Cor.* iii. 16.

The temple of God is holy: which temple ye are. 1 *Cor.* iii. 17.

DEARLY beloved brethren, God, in whom we live and move and have our being, never leaves us, day or night. But the very nearness and custom of his presence hide him from our infirm and sinful hearts; and under cover of this darkness, our inner discernment becomes dim, temptations gain a shameful power, and the good that is in us droops and fades. To clear such blindness away, and recover the pure wisdom of a Christian mind, we are called to this day of remembrance and this house of prayer. Entering here, therefore, we cross the threshold of eternal things, and commune with the Father who seeth in secret. Let us shake off the dust of transitory care, and every disguise that can come between us and God: and, remembering whose disciples we are, come to the simplicity, though it should be also to the sorrows, of Christ.

¶ *The Minister shall then say the following Prayer; all kneeling, and the People responding with ‘* AMEN.’

O GOD, Unsearchable; why are we so blind to thee, who besettest us behind and before? In the daylight of thy constant mercy, we scarcely lift our eye to the infinite heaven whence it flows. Now screen us with thy hand, O Lord, that we may not wait for the night of sorrow, but here, under the shade of holy thought, may learn in what a world we live. Here let us rest from the weary shows of life, and converse with thee, the Only True. And though thou receivest higher praise than ours, from natures that know thee more and serve thee better, yet tune our spirits and join our voices with theirs; and unite us with the faithful and saintly, there and here, in one light of faith, one beauty of holiness, one repose on thee. *Amen.*

> ¶ *Then the Lord's Prayer, to be said by the People after the Minister.*

OUR Father who art in heaven, Hallowed be thy name. Thy kingdom come. Thy will be done on earth, as it is in heaven. Give us this day our daily bread. And forgive us our trespasses, as we forgive them that trespass against us. And lead us not into temptation; but deliver us from evil: For thine is the kingdom, and the power, and the glory, for ever and ever. Amen.

> ¶ *Then shall be said or sung the following Canticle; all standing.*

I WAS glad when my companions said unto me: Come, it is our holy day;

Let us go into the house of the Lord: let us take sweet counsel together;

Let our feet stand within his gates: and heart and voice give thanks unto him.

Blessed be the temple hallowed by his name: pray for peace within its walls,

Peace to young and old that enter there: peace to every soul abiding therein.

For friends' and brethren's sake I will never cease to say: Peace be within thee!

What though for Him who filleth heaven and earth: there can be no dwelling made with hands;

What though his way is in the deep, and his knowledge too wonderful for us: and before him we are as children that cannot speak;

Yet, touched by the altar's living glow: we learn, as an infant, to lisp his name;

And try the wings that beat for his refuge: and flee as a bird to the mountain.

O Lord, when we cry unto thee from the deep: and wait for thee as they that wait for the morning;

Thou wilt have regard to our entreaty: the sigh of the lowly thou wilt not despise.

Not long, O Lord, shall we feel after thee in these courts below: not long wilt thou hearken to these faltering lips.

Our fathers thou hast called to thy higher praise: and gathered to their fathers must all the children be.

Let the dead and living praise thee, O God above, below: let all the generations praise thee.

Let the glorified company of the firstborn: whose names are in the book of life;

Let angels in the height: praise thee, who dwellest in the heavens;

Let thy Church on earth praise thee: the delight of whose Wisdom is in the children of men.

O House of the Lord's praise: Peace be to them that love thee!

If I forget thee: may my right-hand forget its cunning!

To the Only Holy, the First and the Last: be thanksgiving and praise;

From all kindreds and tongues on earth: and the voices of saints in heaven.   Amen.

¶ *Then shall be read the* First Lesson, *taken out of the Old Testament.*

¶ *After that shall be said or sung the following Canticle:*

BLESSED be the Lord God of ages: who never ceaseth to draw more nigh.

His voice in the morning of the world was heard from far: in the evening he speaketh at the door, and entereth to abide with us for ever.

Manifold are thy witnesses, O God, and the angels of thine invisible presence: else had we never known thee.

How should man that is born as the wild-ass's colt stretch his wisdom to thee:—to thee, save to thyself, Unsearchable?

Though thou unsealest the light for all that lives: and lookest through the doors of the shadow of death;

Though thou causest the day-spring to know its place: and sayest to the sea, 'Here shall thy proud waves be stayed;'

Though thou seest the end from the

beginning: and weavest the ages as a work upon the loom;

Yet lo! thou goest by us, and we see thee not: thou passest on also, and we perceive thee not.

> For the days of man are passed, like the swift ships: and his line reacheth not to thee, Eternal!
>
> Till thou didst look for him upon the earth, he was not: and when thou sayest, 'Return,' he is no more.
>
> But thy years are countless as the stars: from everlasting to everlasting thou art God.

Hadst thou not remembered our low estate: and bent to us with thy testimonies from of old;

We had been in darkness and the shadow of death: and the light of thy countenance had been hid.

But the firmament declareth thy glory: the prophets proclaim thy judgments;

The righteous wonder at thy law in their heart: and the songs of Zion make melody to thee.

Lo! these are a part of thy mercies: yet how little a portion is heard of thee!

Blessed be the dawn of thine everlasting light: the fear of the Lord is the beginning of wisdom.

Glory be to God most High: the ever-blessed Father;

Who is, and was, and shall be: world without end. Amen.

¶ *Then shall be read the* SECOND LESSON, *taken out of the New Testament.*

¶ *After that, shall be said or sung the following Canticle:*

LO! at length the True Light:—light for every man born into the world;

Kindling the face of them that receive it: till they become the sons of God.

Cease, blinding glories of the heavens: which none could see and live!

Cease, gross darkness of the earth: where the righteous put forth their hands and fear!

The veil between is taken away: and the mingling day-spring comes;

No longer is the dwelling of Eternal Life too bright above: and the perishable world too dark below.

The Son of God hath dwelt among us: full of grace and truth;

The Son of Man hath gone up on high: made perfect through suffering for the holy of holies.

He is our peace: giving us access by one spirit to the Father;

No more strangers and exiles: but fellow-citizens with the saints, and of the household of God.

O Lord Almighty! we had said of thee: 'Thy thoughts are not as our thoughts;'

But thou hast looked on us as with the pity of a man: and raised us to think the thoughts of God.

We had said, 'Our righteousness reacheth not unto thee: or to the holy ones of thy presence;'

But thou hast made one family, there and

here: one living communion of seen and unseen.

We had said, 'Thou layest men fast in everlasting sleep:' but lo! they sleep into everlasting waking.

Blessed be the Lord God, that giveth beauty for ashes: and the garment of praise for the spirit of heaviness.

Now unto the God of grace: for the might of his Spirit and the love of Christ;

Be glory in the Church throughout all ages: world without end.   Amen.

¶ *Then the Minister shall say the following Prayers; all kneeling, and the People responding with* 'AMEN.'

O GOD, ever blessed and holy! none but the Angels and thy Redeemed can serve thee with a perfect joy. On us, as we look up to the light of thy countenance, the shadows of shameful remembrance fall: and to all thy mercies we must still answer with a cry for more. Called in our measure to be perfect as thou art perfect, we have been most unlike to thee, and are not worthy to be deemed thy children. (Thirsting with momentary desires, we have forsaken the living springs of heavenly wisdom, of which he that drinketh shall never thirst again.) We have been slow to the calls of affection, heedless of the duties, hard under the sorrows, which are thy gracious discipline; yet are oppressed with cares thou layest not on us, with ease thou dost not permit, and wants thou wilt never bless. O Lord, regard our complaint: it is only against our faithless hearts. We have nothing to plead, and renounce our pride before thee. Only leave us not to ourselves. Visit us with the wrestlings of thy Spirit: and lay on us the cross, if we may but grow into the holiness, of Christ. *Amen.*

ETERNAL God, who committest to us the swift and solemn trust of life; since we know not what a day may bring forth, but only that the hour for serving thee is always present, may we wake to the instant claims of thy holy will; not waiting for to-morrow, but yielding to-day. Lay to rest, by the persuasion of thy Spirit, the resistance of our passion, indolence, or fear. Consecrate with thy presence the way our feet may go; and the humblest work will shine, and the roughest places be made plain. Lift us above unrighteous anger and mistrust into faith and hope and charity, by a simple and steadfast reliance on thy sure will: and so may we be modest in our time of wealth, patient under disappointment, ready for danger, serene in death. In all things, draw us to the mind of Christ, that thy lost image may be traced again, and thou mayst own us as at one with him and thee. *Amen.*

O GOD, who leadest us through seasons of life to be partakers of thine eternity; the shadows of our evening hasten on. Quicken us betimes: and spare us that sad word, 'The harvest is past, the summer is ended, and we are not saved.' Anew we dedicate ourselves to thee. We would ask nothing, reserve nothing, for ourselves, save only leave to go whither thou mayst guide, to live not far from thee, and die into thy nearer light. Content to accept the reproach of truth and the self-denials of pure integrity, we would take upon us the yoke of Christ, whom it behoved to suffer ere he entered into his glory.

¶ *In response to this the People shall say:*

Even as he said to all, "If any man come after me, let him deny himself, and take up his cross daily, and follow me."

¶ *In Quires and Places where they sing, here may follow an Anthem or Hymn.*

¶ *Then the following Prayers and Intercessions:*

LORD of all, whose balance trieth the nations, to lift up or to cast down; thou hast planted us, as a people, in quiet resting-places, and stretched out our branches over the sea, and laid upon us a mighty trust. Never through vain conceit may we be blind to the unchanging conditions of thy blessing. The world and its fulness are thine: our portion thereof may we hold, not in wanton self-will, but reverently, as of thee; making it the strong-hold of right, the refuge of the oppressed, and the moderator of lawless ambition. Crown thy servant VICTORIA, our Queen, with every personal and princely blessing. Higher than the eminence of her station raise her by the graces of thy Spirit: and may the glory of her rule be in the simplicity of her obedience. Enrich the members of her house with inward and outward good. Make all who speak or act for this nation true organs of thine equity, that through their wisdom and faithfulness thou mayst be our Lawgiver and Judge. And let it be that, as with the people so with the chiefs, as with the servant so with the master, as with the buyer so with the seller, all may know thee as weighing the path of the just;

that righteousness may be the girdle of our power. *Amen.*

O GOD, who didst send thy word to speak in the Prophets and live in thy Son; and appoint thy Church to be witness of divine things in all the world; revive the purity and deepen the power of its testimony: and through the din of earthly interests and the storm of human passions, let it make the still small voice of thy Spirit inly felt. Nearer and nearer may thy kingdom come from age to age; meeting the face of the young as a rising dawn, and brightening the song of the old, 'Lord, now lettest thou thy servant depart in peace.' Already let its light abash our guilty negligence, and touch with hope each secret sorrow of the earth. By the cleansing spirit of thy Son, make this world a fitting fore-court to that sanctuary not made with hands, where our life is hid with Christ in God. *Amen.*

THE Lord bless us and keep us: may he be gracious unto us; and give us peace now and for evermore. *Amen.* *Numb.* vi. 24–26.

Or

AND now may the peace of God rule in your hearts: and the word of Christ dwell in you richly in all wisdom. *Amen.* *Col.* iii. 15, 16.

Collect for Morning.

ETERNAL God, who hast neither dawn nor evening, yet sendest us alternate mercies of the darkness and the day; there is no light but thine, without, within. As thou liftest the curtain of night from our abodes, take also the veil from all our hearts. Rise with thy morning upon our souls: quicken all our labour and our prayer: and though all else declines, let the noontide of thy grace and peace remain. May we walk, while it is yet day, in the steps of him who, with fewest hours, finished thy divinest work. *Amen.*

Collect for Evening.

O GOD, who faintest not, neither art weary; whose everlasting work is still fresh as thy creative thought; we bless thee for the pity of night and sleep, giving us the rest thou never needest. We would lie down each evening in peace and thankfulness, and commit the folded hours to thee. But, O Lord, through toil and repose, save us from any fatal slumber of the spirit: and keep us through life to the holy vigils of love and service, as they that watch for thy morning of eternity. *Amen.*

A Catalogue of Works

IN

THEOLOGICAL LITERATURE

PUBLISHED BY

MESSRS. LONGMANS, GREEN, & CO.

39 PATERNOSTER ROW, LONDON, E.C.

Abbey and Overton.—THE ENGLISH CHURCH IN THE EIGHTEENTH CENTURY. By CHARLES J. ABBEY, M.A., Rector of Checkendon, Reading, and JOHN H. OVERTON, M.A., Rector of Epworth, Doncaster, Rural Dean of Isle of Axholme. *Crown 8vo.* 7s. 6d.

Adams.—SACRED ALLEGORIES. The Shadow of the Cross—The Distant Hills—The Old Man's Home—The King's Messengers. By the Rev. WILLIAM ADAMS, M.A. *Crown 8vo.* 3s. 6d.

The Four Allegories may be had separately, with Illustrations. 16mo. 1s. each. *Also the Miniature Edition. Four Vols.* 32mo. 1s. each; in a box, 5s.

Aids to the Inner Life.

Edited by the Rev. W. H. HUTCHINGS, M.A., Rector of Kirkby Misperton, Yorkshire. *Five Vols.* 32mo, cloth limp, 6d. each; or cloth extra, 1s. each. *Sold separately.*
Also an Edition *with red borders*, 2s. each.

OF THE IMITATION OF CHRIST. By THOMAS À KEMPIS. In Four Books.

THE CHRISTIAN YEAR.

THE DEVOUT LIFE. By ST. FRANCIS DE SALES.

THE HIDDEN LIFE OF THE SOUL. From the French of JEAN NICOLAS GROU.

THE SPIRITUAL COMBAT. By LAWRENCE SCUPOLI.

Bathe.—Works by the Rev. ANTHONY BATHE, M.A.

A LENT WITH JESUS. A Plain Guide for Churchmen. Containing Readings for Lent and Easter Week, and on the Holy Eucharist. 32mo, 1s.; or in paper cover, 6d.

WHAT I SHOULD BELIEVE. A Simple Manual of Self-Instruction for Church People. *Crown 8vo.* 3s. 6d.

A CATALOGUE OF WORKS

Bickersteth.—Works by EDWARD HENRY BICKERSTETH, D.D., Bishop of Exeter.

THE LORD'S TABLE; or, Meditations on the Holy Communion Office in the Book of Common Prayer. 16mo. 1s.; *or cloth extra*, 2s.

YESTERDAY, TO-DAY, AND FOR EVER: a Poem in Twelve Books. *One Shilling Edition*, 18mo. *With red borders*, 16mo, 2s. 6d. *The Crown 8vo Edition* (5s.) *may still be had.*

Blunt.—Works by the Rev. JOHN HENRY BLUNT, D.D.

THE ANNOTATED BOOK OF COMMON PRAYER: Being an Historical, Ritual, and Theological Commentary on the Devotional System of the Church of England. Edited by the Rev. JOHN HENRY BLUNT, D.D. 4to. 21s.

THE COMPENDIOUS EDITION OF THE ANNOTATED BOOK OF COMMON PRAYER: Forming a concise Commentary on the Devotional System of the Church of England. Edited by the Rev. JOHN HENRY BLUNT, D.D. *Crown 8vo.* 10s. 6d.

DICTIONARY OF DOCTRINAL AND HISTORICAL THEOLOGY. By various Writers. Edited by the Rev. JOHN HENRY BLUNT, D.D. *Imperial 8vo.* 21s.

DICTIONARY OF SECTS, HERESIES, ECCLESIASTICAL PARTIES AND SCHOOLS OF RELIGIOUS THOUGHT. By various Writers. Edited by the Rev. JOHN HENRY BLUNT, D.D. *Imperial 8vo.* 21s.

THE BOOK OF CHURCH LAW. Being an Exposition of the Legal Rights and Duties of the Parochial Clergy and the Laity of the Church of England. Revised by Sir WALTER G. F. PHILLIMORE, Bart., D.C.L. *Crown 8vo.* 7s. 6d.

A COMPANION TO THE BIBLE: Being a Plain Commentary on Scripture History, to the end of the Apostolic Age. *Two vols. small 8vo. Sold separately.*

THE OLD TESTAMENT. 3s. 6d.   THE NEW TESTAMENT. 3s. 6d.

HOUSEHOLD THEOLOGY: a Handbook of Religious Information respecting the Holy Bible, the Prayer Book, the Church, the Ministry, Divine Worship, the Creeds, etc. etc. *Paper cover*, 16mo. 1s. Also the Larger Edition, 3s. 6d.

Body.—Works by the Rev. GEORGE BODY, D.D., Canon of Durham.

THE SCHOOL OF CALVARY; or, Laws of Christian Life revealed from the Cross. A Course of Lectures delivered in substance at All Saints', Margaret Street. *Small 8vo.* 3s. 6d.

THE LIFE OF JUSTIFICATION: a Series of Lectures delivered in substance at All Saints', Margaret Street. 16mo. 2s. 6d.

THE LIFE OF TEMPTATION: a Course of Lectures delivered in substance at St. Peter's, Eaton Square; also at All Saints', Margaret Street. 16mo. 2s. 6d.

Boultbee.—A COMMENTARY ON THE THIRTY-NINE ARTICLES OF THE CHURCH OF ENGLAND. By the Rev. T. P. BOULTBEE, formerly Principal of the London College of Divinity, St. John's Hall, Highbury. *Crown 8vo.* 6s.

Bright.—Works by WILLIAM BRIGHT, D.D., Canon of Christ Church, Oxford.

LESSONS FROM THE LIVES OF THREE GREAT FATHERS: St. Athanasius, St. Chrysostom, and St. Augustine. *Crown 8vo.* 6s.

THE INCARNATION AS A MOTIVE POWER. *Crown 8vo.* 6s.

FAITH AND LIFE: Readings for the greater Holy Days, and the Sundays from Advent to Trinity. Compiled from Ancient Writers. *Small 8vo.* 5s.

IONA AND OTHER VERSES. *Small 8vo.* 4s. 6d.

HYMNS AND OTHER VERSES. *Small 8vo.* 5s.

Bright and Medd.—LIBER PRECUM PUBLICARUM ECCLESIÆ ANGLICANÆ. A GULIELMO BRIGHT, S.T.P., et PETRO GOLDSMITH MEDD, A.M., Latine redditus. [In hac Editione continentur Versiones Latinæ—1. Libri Precum Publicarum Ecclesiæ Anglicanæ; 2. Liturgiæ Primæ Reformatæ; 3. Liturgiæ Scoticanæ; 4. Liturgiæ Americanæ.] *Small 8vo.* 7s. 6d.

Browne.—AN EXPOSITION OF THE THIRTY-NINE ARTICLES, Historical and Doctrinal. By E. H. BROWNE, D.D., formerly Bishop of Winchester. *8vo.* 16s.

Campion and Beamont.—THE PRAYER BOOK INTERLEAVED. With Historical Illustrations and Explanatory Notes arranged parallel to the Text. By W. M. CAMPION, D.D., and W. J. BEAMONT, M.A. *Small 8vo.* 7s. 6d.

Carter.—Works edited by the Rev. T. T. CARTER, M.A., Hon. Canon of Christ Church, Oxford.

THE TREASURY OF DEVOTION: a Manual of Prayer for General and Daily Use. Compiled by a Priest. *18mo.* 2s. 6d.; *cloth limp*, 2s.; *or bound with the Book of Common Prayer*, 3s. 6d. *Large-Type Edition. Crown 8vo.* 3s. 6d.

THE WAY OF LIFE: A Book of Prayers and Instruction for the Young at School, with a Preparation for Confirmation. Compiled by a Priest. *18mo.* 1s. 6d.

THE PATH OF HOLINESS: a First Book of Prayers, with the Service of the Holy Communion, for the Young. Compiled by a Priest. With Illustrations. *16mo.* 1s. 6d.; *cloth limp*, 1s.

THE GUIDE TO HEAVEN: a Book of Prayers for every Want. (For the Working Classes.) Compiled by a Priest. *18mo.* 1s. 6d.; *cloth limp*, 1s. *Large-Type Edition. Crown 8vo.* 1s. 6d.; *cloth limp*, 1s.

[continued.

Carter.—Works edited by the Rev. T. T. CARTER, M.A., Hon. Canon of Christ Church, Oxford—*continued.*
    SELF-RENUNCIATION. 16mo. 2s. 6d. *Also the Larger Edition.* *Small 8vo.* 3s. 6d.
    THE STAR OF CHILDHOOD; a First Book of Prayers and Instruction for Children. Compiled by a Priest. With Illustrations. 16mo. 2s. 6d.

Carter.—MAXIMS AND GLEANINGS FROM THE WRITINGS OF T. T. CARTER, M.A. Selected and arranged for Daily Use. *Crown 16mo.* 1s.

Chandler.—THE SPIRIT OF MAN: An Essay in Christian Philosophy. By the Rev. A. CHANDLER, M.A., Rector of Poplar, E. *Crown 8vo.* 5s.

Conybeare and Howson.—THE LIFE AND EPISTLES OF ST. PAUL. By the Rev. W. J. CONYBEARE, M.A., and the Very Rev. J. S. HOWSON, D.D. With numerous Maps and Illustrations.
    LIBRARY EDITION. *Two Vols. 8vo.* 21s.
    STUDENT'S EDITION. *One Vol. Crown 8vo.* 6s.

Crake.—HISTORY OF THE CHURCH UNDER THE ROMAN EMPIRE, A.D. 30-476. By the Rev. A. D. CRAKE, B.A. *Crown 8vo.* 7s. 6d.

Devotional Series, 16mo, Red Borders. *Each* 2s. 6d.
    BICKERSTETH'S YESTERDAY, TO-DAY, AND FOR EVER.
    CHILCOT'S TREATISE ON EVIL THOUGHTS.
    THE CHRISTIAN YEAR.
    DEVOTIONAL BIRTHDAY BOOK.
    HERBERT'S POEMS AND PROVERBS.
    KEMPIS' (À) OF THE IMITATION OF CHRIST.
    ST. FRANCIS DE SALES' THE DEVOUT LIFE.
    WILSON'S THE LORD'S SUPPER. *Large type.*
    *TAYLOR'S (JEREMY) HOLY LIVING.
    * ——— ——— HOLY DYING.
        * *These two in one Volume.* 5s.

Devotional Series, 18mo, without Red Borders. *Each* 1s.
    BICKERSTETH'S YESTERDAY, TO-DAY, AND FOR EVER.
    THE CHRISTIAN YEAR.
    HERBERT'S POEMS AND PROVERBS.
    KEMPIS' (À) OF THE IMITATION OF CHRIST.
    ST. FRANCIS DE SALES' THE DEVOUT LIFE.
    WILSON'S THE LORD'S SUPPER. *Large type.*
    *TAYLOR'S (JEREMY) HOLY LIVING.
    * ——— ——— HOLY DYING.
        * *These two in one Volume.* 2s. 6d.

Edersheim.—Works by ALFRED EDERSHEIM, M.A., D.D., Ph.D., sometime Grinfield Lecturer on the Septuagint, Oxford.

 THE LIFE AND TIMES OF JESUS THE MESSIAH. *Two Vols.* 8vo. 24s.

 JESUS THE MESSIAH: being an Abridged Edition of 'The Life and Times of Jesus the Messiah.' *Crown 8vo.* 7s. 6d.

 PROPHECY AND HISTORY IN RELATION TO THE MESSIAH: The Warburton Lectures, 1880-1884. 8vo. 12s.

 TOHU-VA-VOHU ('Without Form and Void'): being a collection of Fragmentary Thoughts and Criticism. *Crown 8vo.* 6s.

Ellicott.—Works by C. J. ELLICOTT, D.D., Bishop of Gloucester and Bristol.

 A CRITICAL AND GRAMMATICAL COMMENTARY ON ST. PAUL'S EPISTLES. Greek Text, with a Critical and Grammatical Commentary, and a Revised English Translation. 8vo.

  1 CORINTHIANS. 16s.
  GALATIANS. 8s. 6d.
  EPHESIANS. 8s. 6d.
  PASTORAL EPISTLES. 10s. 6d.
  PHILIPPIANS, COLOSSIANS, AND PHILEMON. 10s. 6d.
  THESSALONIANS. 7s. 6d.

 HISTORICAL LECTURES ON THE LIFE OF OUR LORD JESUS CHRIST. 8vo. 12s.

Epochs of Church History. Edited by MANDELL CREIGHTON, D.D., LL.D., Bishop of Peterborough. *Fcap. 8vo.* 2s. 6d. each.

THE ENGLISH CHURCH IN OTHER LANDS. By the Rev. H. W. TUCKER, M.A.

THE HISTORY OF THE REFORMATION IN ENGLAND. By the Rev. GEO. G. PERRY, M.A.

THE CHURCH OF THE EARLY FATHERS. By the Rev. ALFRED PLUMMER, D.D.

THE EVANGELICAL REVIVAL IN THE EIGHTEENTH CENTURY. By the Rev. J. H. OVERTON, M.A.

THE UNIVERSITY OF OXFORD. By the Hon. G. C. BRODRICK, D.C.L.

THE UNIVERSITY OF CAMBRIDGE. By J. BASS MULLINGER, M.A.

THE ENGLISH CHURCH IN THE MIDDLE AGES. By the Rev. W. HUNT, M.A.

THE CHURCH AND THE EASTERN EMPIRE. By the Rev. H. F. TOZER, M.A.

THE CHURCH AND THE ROMAN EMPIRE. By the Rev. A. CARR.

THE CHURCH AND THE PURITANS, 1570-1660. By HENRY OFFLEY WAKEMAN, M.A.

HILDEBRAND AND HIS TIMES. By the Rev. W. R. W. STEPHENS, M.A.

THE POPES AND THE HOHENSTAUFEN. By UGO BALZANI.

THE COUNTER-REFORMATION. By ADOLPHUS WILLIAM WARD, Litt. D.

WYCLIFFE AND MOVEMENTS FOR REFORM. By REGINALD L. POOLE, M.A.

THE ARIAN CONTROVERSY. By H. M. GWATKIN, M.A.

Fosbery.—Works edited by the Rev. THOMAS VINCENT FOSBERY, M.A., sometime Vicar of St. Giles's, Reading.

VOICES OF COMFORT. *Cheap Edition. Small 8vo.* 3s. 6d.
The Larger Edition (7s. 6d.) *may still be had.*

HYMNS AND POEMS FOR THE SICK AND SUFFERING. In connection with the Service for the Visitation of the Sick. Selected from Various Authors. *Small 8vo.* 3s. 6d.

Garland.—THE PRACTICAL TEACHING OF THE APOCALYPSE. By the Rev. G. V. GARLAND, M.A. 8vo. 16s.

Gore.—Works by the Rev. CHARLES GORE, M.A., Principal of the Pusey House; Fellow of Trinity College, Oxford.

THE MINISTRY OF THE CHRISTIAN CHURCH. 8vo. 10s. 6d.
ROMAN CATHOLIC CLAIMS. *Crown 8vo.* 3s. 6d.

Goulburn.—Works by EDWARD MEYRICK GOULBURN, D.D., D.C.L., sometime Dean of Norwich.

THOUGHTS ON PERSONAL RELIGION. *Small 8vo,* 6s. 6d.; *Cheap Edition,* 3s. 6d.; *Presentation Edition,* 2 vols. *small 8vo,* 10s. 6d.

THE PURSUIT OF HOLINESS: a Sequel to 'Thoughts on Personal Religion.' *Small 8vo.* 5s. *Cheap Edition,* 3s. 6d.

THE CHILD SAMUEL: a Practical and Devotional Commentary on the Birth and Childhood of the Prophet Samuel, as recorded in 1 Sam. i., ii. 1-27, iii. *Small 8vo.* 2s. 6d.

THE GOSPEL OF THE CHILDHOOD: a Practical and Devotional Commentary on the Single Incident of our Blessed Lord's Childhood (St. Luke ii. 41 to the end). *Crown 8vo.* 2s. 6d.

THE COLLECTS OF THE DAY: an Exposition, Critical and Devotional, of the Collects appointed at the Communion. With Preliminary Essays on their Structure, Sources, etc. 2 vols. *Crown 8vo.* 8s. each.

THOUGHTS UPON THE LITURGICAL GOSPELS for the Sundays, one for each day in the year. With an Introduction on their Origin, History, the Modifications made in them by the Reformers and by the Revisers of the Prayer Book. 2 vols. *Crown 8vo.* 16s.

MEDITATIONS UPON THE LITURGICAL GOSPELS for the Minor Festivals of Christ, the two first Week-days of the Easter and Whitsun Festivals, and the Red-letter Saints' Days. *Crown 8vo.* 8s. 6d.

FAMILY PRAYERS compiled from various sources (chiefly from Bishop Hamilton's Manual), and arranged on the Liturgical Principle. *Crown 8vo.* 3s. 6d. *Cheap Edition.* 16mo. 1s.

Harrison.—PROBLEMS OF CHRISTIANITY AND SCEPTICISM; Lessons from Twenty Years' Experience in the Field of Christian Evidence. By the Rev. ALEXANDER J. HARRISON, B.D., Lecturer of the Christian Evidence Society. *Crown 8vo.* 7s. 6d.

Hernaman.—LYRA CONSOLATIONIS. From the Poets of the Seventeenth, Eighteenth, and Nineteenth Centuries. Selected and arranged by CLAUDIA FRANCES HERNAMAN. *Small 8vo. 6s.*

Holland.—Works by the Rev. HENRY SCOTT HOLLAND, M.A., Canon and Precentor of St. Paul's.
- CREED AND CHARACTER: Sermons. *Crown 8vo. 7s. 6d.*
- ON BEHALF OF BELIEF. Sermons preached in St. Paul's Cathedral. *Crown 8vo. 6s.*
- CHRIST OR ECCLESIASTES. Sermons preached in St. Paul's Cathedral. *Crown 8vo. 3s. 6d.*
- GOOD FRIDAY. Being Addresses on the Seven Last Words, delivered at St. Paul's Cathedral on Good Friday. *Small 8vo. 2s.*
- LOGIC AND LIFE, with other Sermons. *Crown 8vo. 7s. 6d.*

Hopkins.—CHRIST THE CONSOLER. A Book of Comfort for the Sick. By ELLICE HOPKINS. *Small 8vo. 2s. 6d.*

Ingram.—HAPPINESS: In the Spiritual Life; or, 'The Secret of the Lord.' A Series of Practical Considerations. By the Rev. W. CLAVELL INGRAM, M.A., Vicar of St. Matthew's, Leicester. *Crown 8vo. 7s. 6d.*

INHERITANCE, THE, OF THE SAINTS; or, Thoughts on the Communion of Saints and the Life of the World to come. Collected chiefly from English Writers by L. P. With a Preface by the Rev. HENRY SCOTT HOLLAND, M.A. *Crown 8vo. 7s. 6d.*

Jameson.—Works by Mrs. JAMESON.
- SACRED AND LEGENDARY ART, containing Legends of the Angels and Archangels, the Evangelists, the Apostles. With 19 etchings and 187 Woodcuts. *Two Vols. Cloth, gilt top, 20s. net.*
- LEGENDS OF THE MONASTIC ORDERS, as represented in the Fine Arts. With 11 etchings and 88 Woodcuts. *One Vol. Cloth, gilt top, 10s. net.*
- LEGENDS OF THE MADONNA, OR BLESSED VIRGIN MARY. With 27 Etchings and 165 Woodcuts. *One Vol. Cloth, gilt top, 10s. net.*
- THE HISTORY OF OUR LORD, as exemplified in Works of Art. Commenced by the late Mrs. JAMESON; continued and completed by LADY EASTLAKE. With 31 etchings and 281 Woodcuts. *Two Vols. 8vo. 20s. net.*

Jennings.—ECCLESIA ANGLICANA. A History of the Church of Christ in England from the Earliest to the Present Times. By the Rev. ARTHUR CHARLES JENNINGS, M.A. *Crown 8vo. 7s. 6d.*

Jukes.—Works by ANDREW JUKES.
>THE NEW MAN AND THE ETERNAL LIFE. Notes on the Reiterated Amens of the Son of God. *Crown 8vo.* 6s.
>THE NAMES OF GOD IN HOLY SCRIPTURE: a Revelation of His Nature and Relationships. *Crown 8vo.* 4s. 6d.
>THE TYPES OF GENESIS. *Crown 8vo.* 7s. 6d.
>THE SECOND DEATH AND THE RESTITUTION OF ALL THINGS. *Crown 8vo.* 3s. 6d.
>THE MYSTERY OF THE KINGDOM. *Crown 8vo.* 2s. 6d.

Keble.—MAXIMS AND GLEANINGS FROM THE WRITINGS OF JOHN KEBLE, M.A. Selected and Arranged for Daily Use. By C. M. S. *Crown 16mo.* 1s.
>SELECTIONS FROM THE WRITINGS OF JOHN KEBLE, M.A. *Crown 8vo.* 3s. 6d.

Kennaway.—CONSOLATIO; OR, COMFORT FOR THE AFFLICTED. Edited by the late Rev. C. E. KENNAWAY. *16mo.* 2s. 6d.

King.—DR. LIDDON'S TOUR IN EGYPT AND PALESTINE IN 1886. Being Letters descriptive of the Tour, written by his Sister, Mrs. KING. *Crown 8vo.* 5s.

Knox Little.—Works by W. J. KNOX LITTLE, M.A., Canon Residentiary of Worcester, and Vicar of Hoar Cross.
>THE CHRISTIAN HOME. *Crown 8vo.* 6s. 6d.
>THE HOPES AND DECISIONS OF THE PASSION OF OUR MOST HOLY REDEEMER. *Crown 8vo.* 3s. 6d.
>THE THREE HOURS' AGONY OF OUR BLESSED REDEEMER. Being Addresses in the form of Meditations delivered in St. Alban's Church, Manchester, on Good Friday. *Small 8vo.* 2s.; *or in Paper Cover,* 1s.
>CHARACTERISTICS AND MOTIVES OF THE CHRISTIAN LIFE. Ten Sermons preached in Manchester Cathedral, in Lent and Advent. *Crown 8vo.* 3s. 6d.
>SERMONS PREACHED FOR THE MOST PART IN MANCHESTER. *Crown 8vo.* 3s. 6d.
>THE MYSTERY OF THE PASSION OF OUR MOST HOLY REDEEMER. *Crown 8vo.* 3s. 6d.
>THE WITNESS OF THE PASSION OF OUR MOST HOLY REDEEMER. *Crown 8vo.* 3s. 6d.
>THE LIGHT OF LIFE. Sermons preached on Various Occasions. *Crown 8vo.* 3s. 6d.
>SUNLIGHT AND SHADOW IN THE CHRISTIAN LIFE. Sermons preached for the most part in America. *Crown 8vo.* 3s. 6d.

IN THEOLOGICAL LITERATURE. 9

Lear.—Works by, and Edited by, H. L. SIDNEY LEAR.

FOR DAYS AND YEARS. A Book containing a Text, Short Reading, and Hymn for Every Day in the Church's Year. 16mo. 2s. 6d. *Also a Cheap Edition*, 32mo. 1s.; *or cloth gilt*, 1s. 6d.

FIVE MINUTES. Daily Readings of Poetry 16mo. 3s. 6d. *Also a Cheap Edition.* 32mo. 1s.; *or cloth gilt*, 1s. 6d.

WEARINESS. A Book for the Languid and Lonely. *Large Type. Small 8vo.* 5s.

THE LIGHT OF THE CONSCIENCE. 16mo. 2s. 6d. 32mo. 1s.; *cloth limp*, 6d.

CHRISTIAN BIOGRAPHIES. *Nine Vols. Crown 8vo. 3s. 6d. each.*

MADAME LOUISE DE FRANCE, Daughter of Louis XV., known also as the Mother Térèse de St. Augustin.

A DOMINICAN ARTIST: a Sketch of the Life of the Rev. Père Besson, of the Order of St. Dominic.

HENRI PERREYVE. By A. GRATRY.

ST. FRANCIS DE SALES, Bishop and Prince of Geneva.

THE REVIVAL OF PRIESTLY LIFE IN THE SEVENTEENTH CENTURY IN FRANCE.

A CHRISTIAN PAINTER OF THE NINETEENTH CENTURY.

BOSSUET AND HIS CONTEMPORARIES.

FÉNELON, ARCHBISHOP OF CAMBRAI.

HENRI DOMINIQUE LACORDAIRE.

DEVOTIONAL WORKS. Edited by H. L. SIDNEY LEAR. *New and Uniform Editions. Nine Vols.* 16mo. 2s. 6d. each.

FÉNELON'S SPIRITUAL LETTERS TO MEN.

FÉNELON'S SPIRITUAL LETTERS TO WOMEN.

A SELECTION FROM THE SPIRITUAL LETTERS OF ST. FRANCIS DE SALES.

THE SPIRIT OF ST. FRANCIS DE SALES.

THE HIDDEN LIFE OF THE SOUL.

THE LIGHT OF THE CONSCIENCE.

SELF-RENUNCIATION. From the French.

ST. FRANCIS DE SALES' OF THE LOVE OF GOD.

SELECTIONS FROM PASCAL'S THOUGHTS.

Library of Spiritual Works for English Catholics. *Original Edition. With Red Borders. Small 8vo. 5s. each. New and Cheaper Editions.* 16mo. 2s. 6d. each.

OF THE IMITATION OF CHRIST.

THE SPIRITUAL COMBAT. By LAURENCE SCUPOLI.

THE DEVOUT LIFE. By ST. FRANCIS DE SALES.

OF THE LOVE OF GOD. By ST. FRANCIS DE SALES.

THE CONFESSIONS OF ST. AUGUSTINE. *In Ten Books.*

THE CHRISTIAN YEAR. 5s. *Edition only*

Mozley.—Works by J. B. MOZLEY, D.D., late Canon of Christ Church, and Regius Professor of Divinity at Oxford.

ESSAYS, HISTORICAL AND THEOLOGICAL. *Two Vols.* 8vo. 24s.

EIGHT LECTURES ON MIRACLES. Being the Bampton Lectures for 1865. *Crown 8vo. 7s. 6d.*

RULING IDEAS IN EARLY AGES AND THEIR RELATION TO OLD TESTAMENT FAITH. Lectures delivered to Graduates of the University of Oxford. 8vo. 10s. 6d.

SERMONS PREACHED BEFORE THE UNIVERSITY OF OXFORD, and on Various Occasions. *Crown 8vo. 7s. 6d.*

SERMONS, PAROCHIAL AND OCCASIONAL. *Crown 8vo. 7s. 6d.*

Mozley.—Works by the Rev. T. MOZLEY, M.A., Author of 'Reminiscences of Oriel College and the Oxford Movement.'

THE WORD. *Crown 8vo. 7s. 6d.*

THE SON. *Crown 8vo. 7s. 6d.*

LETTERS FROM ROME ON THE OCCASION OF THE ŒCUMENICAL COUNCIL 1869-1870. *Two Vols. Cr. 8vo.* 18s.

Newbolt.—Works by the Rev. W. C. E. NEWBOLT, M.A., Canon Residentiary of St. Paul's.

THE FRUIT OF THE SPIRIT. Being Ten Addresses bearing on the Spiritual Life. *Crown 8vo. 2s. 6d.*

THE MAN OF GOD. Being Six Addresses delivered during Lent 1886, at the Primary Ordination of the Right Rev. the Lord Alwyne Compton, D.D., Bishop of Ely. *Small 8vo. 1s. 6d.*

THE VOICE OF THE PRAYER BOOK. Being Spiritual Addresses bearing on the Book of Common Prayer. *Crown 8vo. 2s. 6d.*

Newnham.—THE ALL-FATHER: Sermons preached in a Village Church. By the Rev. H. P. NEWNHAM. With Preface by EDNA LYALL. *Crown 8vo. 4s. 6d.*

Newnham.—ALRESFORD ESSAYS FOR THE TIMES. By Rev. W. O. NEWNHAM, M.A., late Rector of Alresford. CONTENTS:—Bible Story of Creation—Bible Story of Eden—Bible Story of the Deluge—After Death—Miracles: A Conversation—Eternal Punishment—The Resurrection of the Body. *Crown 8vo. 6s.*

Newman.—Works by JOHN HENRY NEWMAN, B.D., sometime Vicar of St. Mary's, Oxford.

PAROCHIAL AND PLAIN SERMONS. *Eight Vols. Cabinet Edition. Crown 8vo. 5s. each. Popular Edition. Eight Vols. Crown 8vo. 3s. 6d. each.*

SELECTION, ADAPTED TO THE SEASONS OF THE ECCLESIASTICAL YEAR, from the 'Parochial and Plain Sermons.' *Cabinet Edition. Crown 8vo. 5s. Popular Edition. Crown 8vo. 3s. 6d.*

FIFTEEN SERMONS PREACHED BEFORE THE UNIVERSITY OF OXFORD, between A.D. 1826 and 1843. *Crown 8vo. 5s.*

SERMONS BEARING UPON SUBJECTS OF THE DAY. *Cabinet Edition. Crown 8vo. 5s. Popular Edition. Crown 8vo. 3s. 6d.*

LECTURES ON THE DOCTRINE OF JUSTIFICATION. *Crown 8vo. 5s.*

THE LETTERS AND CORRESPONDENCE OF JOHN HENRY NEWMAN DURING HIS LIFE IN THE ENGLISH CHURCH. With a Brief Autobiographical Memoir. Arranged and Edited by ANNE MOZLEY. *Two Vols. 8vo. 30s. net.*

*** *For other Works by Cardinal Newman, see Messrs. Longmans & Co.'s Catalogue of Works in General Literature.*

Osborne.—Works by EDWARD OSBORNE, Mission Priest of the Society of St. John the Evangelist, Cowley, Oxford.

THE CHILDREN'S SAVIOUR. Instructions to Children on the Life of our Lord and Saviour Jesus Christ. *Illustrated. 16mo. 2s. 6d.*

THE SAVIOUR-KING. Instructions to Children on Old Testament Types and Illustrations of the Life of Christ. *Illustrated. 16mo. 2s. 6d.*

THE CHILDREN'S FAITH. Instructions to Children on the Apostles' Creed. *Illustrated. 16mo. 2s. 6d.*

Oxenden.—Works by the Right Rev. ASHTON OXENDEN, formerly Bishop of Montreal.

THE HISTORY OF MY LIFE: An Autobiography. *Crown 8vo. 5s.*

PEACE AND ITS HINDRANCES. *Crown 8vo. 1s.; sewed, 2s., cloth.*

THE PATHWAY OF SAFETY; or, Counsel to the Awakened. *Fcap. 8vo, large type. 2s. 6d. Cheap Edition. Small type, limp. 1s.*

THE EARNEST COMMUNICANT. *New Red Rubric Edition. 32mo, cloth. 2s. Common Edition. 32mo, 1s.*

OUR CHURCH AND HER SERVICES. *Fcap. 8vo. 2s. 6d.*

[continued.

Oxenden.—Works by the Right Rev. ASHTON OXENDEN, formerly Bishop of Montreal—*continued*.

    FAMILY PRAYERS FOR FOUR WEEKS. First Series. *Fcap. 8vo.* 2s. 6d. Second Series. *Fcap. 8vo.* 2s. 6d.
        LARGE TYPE EDITION. Two Series in one Volume. *Crown 8vo.* 6s.

    COTTAGE SERMONS; or, Plain Words to the Poor. *Fcap. 8vo.* 2s. 6d.

    THOUGHTS FOR HOLY WEEK. *16mo, cloth.* 1s. 6d.

    DECISION. *18mo.* 1s. 6d.

    THE HOME BEYOND; or, A Happy Old Age. *Fcap. 8vo.* 1s. 6d.

    THE LABOURING MAN'S BOOK. *18mo, large type, cloth.* 1s. 6d.

Paget.—Works by FRANCIS PAGET, D.D., Dean of Christ Church, Oxford.

    THE SPIRIT OF DISCIPLINE: Sermons. *Crown 8vo.* 6s. 6d.

    FACULTIES AND DIFFICULTIES FOR BELIEF AND DISBELIEF. *Crown 8vo.* 6s. 6d.

    THE HALLOWING OF WORK. Addresses given at Eton, January 16-18, 1888. *Small 8vo.* 2s.

PRACTICAL REFLECTIONS. By a CLERGYMAN. With Prefaces by H. P. LIDDON, D.D., D.C.L. *Crown 8vo.*

        Vol. I.—THE HOLY GOSPELS. 4s. 6d.
        Vol. II.—ACTS TO REVELATION. 6s.
        THE PSALMS. 5s.

PRIEST (THE) TO THE ALTAR; Or, Aids to the Devout Celebration of Holy Communion, chiefly after the Ancient English Use of Sarum. *Royal 8vo.* 12s.

Pusey.—Works by E. B. PUSEY, D.D.

    PRIVATE PRAYERS. With Preface by H. P. LIDDON, D.D. *32mo.* 1s.

    PRAYERS FOR A YOUNG SCHOOLBOY. With a Preface by H. P. LIDDON, D.D. *24mo.* 1s.

    SELECTIONS FROM THE WRITINGS OF EDWARD BOUVERIE PUSEY, D.D. *Crown 8vo.* 3s. 6d.

    MAXIMS AND GLEANINGS FROM THE WRITINGS OF EDWARD BOUVERIE PUSEY, D.D. Selected and Arranged for Daily Use. By C. M. S. *Crown 16mo.* 1s.

Reynolds.—THE NATURAL HISTORY OF IMMORTALITY. By the Rev. J. W. REYNOLDS, M.A., Prebendary of St. Paul's. *Crown 8vo.* 7s. 6d.

Richmond.—CHRISTIAN ECONOMICS. By the Rev. WILFRID RICHMOND, M.A., sometime Warden of Trinity College, Glenalmond. *Crown 8vo.* 6s.

Sanday.—THE ORACLES OF GOD: Nine Lectures on the Nature and Extent of Biblical Inspiration and the Special Significance of the Old Testament Scriptures at the Present Time. By W. SANDAY, M.A., D.D., LL.D., Dean Ireland's Professor of Exegesis and Fellow of Exeter College. *Crown 8vo.* 4s.

Seebohm.—THE OXFORD REFORMERS—JOHN COLET, ERASMUS, AND THOMAS MORE: A History of their Fellow-Work. By FREDERIC SEEBOHM. *8vo.* 14s.

Stanton.—THE PLACE OF AUTHORITY IN MATTERS OF RELIGIOUS BELIEF. By VINCENT HENRY STANTON, D.D., Fellow of Trinity College, Ely Professor of Divinity, Cambridge. *Crown 8vo.* 6s.

Stephen.—ESSAYS IN ECCLESIASTICAL BIOGRAPHY. By the Right Hon. Sir J. STEPHEN. *Crown 8vo.* 7s. 6d.

Swayne.—THE BLESSED DEAD IN PARADISE. Four All Saints' Day Sermons, preached in Salisbury Cathedral. By R. G. SWAYNE, M.A. *Crown 8vo.* 3s. 6d.

Tweddell.—THE SOUL IN CONFLICT. A Practical Examination of some Difficulties and Duties of the Spiritual Life. By MARSHALL TWEDDELL, M.A., Vicar of St. Saviour, Paddington. *Crown 8vo.* 6s.

Twells.—COLLOQUIES ON PREACHING. By HENRY TWELLS, M.A., Honorary Canon of Peterborough. *Crown 8vo.* 5s.

Wakeman.—THE HISTORY OF RELIGION IN ENGLAND. By HENRY OFFLEY WAKEMAN, M.A. *Small 8vo.* 1s. 6d.

Welldon.—THE FUTURE AND THE PAST. Sermons preached to Harrow Boys. By the Rev. J. E. C. WELLDON, M.A., Head Master of Harrow School. *Crown 8vo.* 7s. 6d.

Williams.—Works by the Rev. ISAAC WILLIAMS, B.D.

    A DEVOTIONAL COMMENTARY ON THE GOSPEL NARRATIVE. *Eight Vols. Crown 8vo.* 5s. each. *Sold separately.*

THOUGHTS ON THE STUDY OF THE HOLY GOSPELS.	OUR LORD'S MINISTRY (Third Year).
A HARMONY OF THE FOUR GOSPELS.	THE HOLY WEEK.
OUR LORD'S NATIVITY.	OUR LORD'S PASSION.
OUR LORD'S MINISTRY (Second Year).	OUR LORD'S RESURRECTION.

    FEMALE CHARACTERS OF HOLY SCRIPTURE. A Series of Sermons. *Crown 8vo.* 5s.

[continued.

Williams.—Works by the Rev. ISAAC WILLIAMS, B.D., formerly Fellow of Trinity College, Oxford—*continued.*

THE CHARACTERS OF THE OLD TESTAMENT. A Series of Sermons. *Crown 8vo. 5s.*

THE APOCALYPSE. With Notes and Reflections. *Crown 8vo. 5s.*

SERMONS ON THE EPISTLES AND GOSPELS FOR THE SUNDAYS AND HOLY DAYS THROUGHOUT THE YEAR. *Two Vols. Crown 8vo. 5s. each.*

PLAIN SERMONS ON THE CATECHISM. *Two Vols. Crown 8vo. 5s. each.*

SELECTIONS FROM THE WRITINGS OF ISAAC WILLIAMS, B.D. *Crown 8vo. 3s. 6d.*

Woodford.—Works by JAMES RUSSELL WOODFORD, D.D., sometime Lord Bishop of Ely.

THE GREAT COMMISSION. Twelve Addresses on the Ordinal. Edited, with an Introduction on the Ordinations of his Episcopate, by HERBERT MORTIMER LUCKOCK, D.D. *Crown 8vo. 5s.*

SERMONS ON OLD AND NEW TESTAMENT SUBJECTS. Edited by HERBERT MORTIMER LUCKOCK, D.D. *Crown 8vo. 5s.*

Woodruff.—THE CHILDREN'S YEAR. Verses for the Sundays and Holy Days throughout the Year. By C. H. WOODRUFF, B.C.L. With an Introduction by the LORD BISHOP OF SOUTHWELL. *Fcap. 8vo. 3s. 6d.*

Wordsworth.

For List of Works by the late Christopher Wordsworth, D.D., Bishop of Lincoln, see Messrs. Longmans & Co.'s Catalogue of Theological Works, 32 pp. Sent post free on application.

Wordsworth.—Works by ELIZABETH WORDSWORTH, Principal of Lady Margaret Hall, Oxford.

ILLUSTRATIONS OF THE CREED. *Crown 8vo. 5s.*

CHRISTOPHER AND OTHER POEMS. *Crown 8vo. 6s.*

Younghusband.—Works by FRANCES YOUNGHUSBAND.

THE STORY OF OUR LORD, told in Simple Language for Children. With 25 Illustrations from Pictures by the Old Masters. *Crown 8vo. 2s. 6d.*

THE STORY OF GENESIS, told in Simple Language for Children. *Crown 8vo. 2s. 6d.*

THE STORY OF THE EXODUS, told in Simple Language for Children. With Map and 29 Illustrations. *Crown 8vo. 2s. 6d.*

Printed by T. and A. CONSTABLE, Printers to Her Majesty,
at the Edinburgh University Press.

20,000/12/91.

www.ingramcontent.com/pod-product-compliance
Lightning Source LLC
Chambersburg PA
CBHW030256170426
43202CB00009B/768